GRAFFITI VERITE' 16 (GV16)
Special 1974 Commemorative Reissue

I0473731

IMPRESSIONS

A BLACK ARTS AND CULTURE MAGAZINE

Volume 1 Number 1
Original Publication: December 1974

Reissue for Educational & Historical Reference Use Only

Disclaimer:
All Promotional Advertisements, Store Addresses, Events, Telephone Numbers, Magazine Location, Product Sale Prices and Magazine Subscription information within the Original 1974 issue are no longer, in most cases, in existence and/or applicable.

Please direct all inquires regarding the Special 1974 Commemorative Reissue of the GV16 IMPRESSIONS MAGAZINE (2012) to:

IMPRESSIONS MAGAZINE

c/o BRYAN WORLD PRODUCTIONS
P.O. Box 74033 Los Angeles, CA 90004 USA
website: www.graffitiverite.com
e-mail: bryworld@aol.com

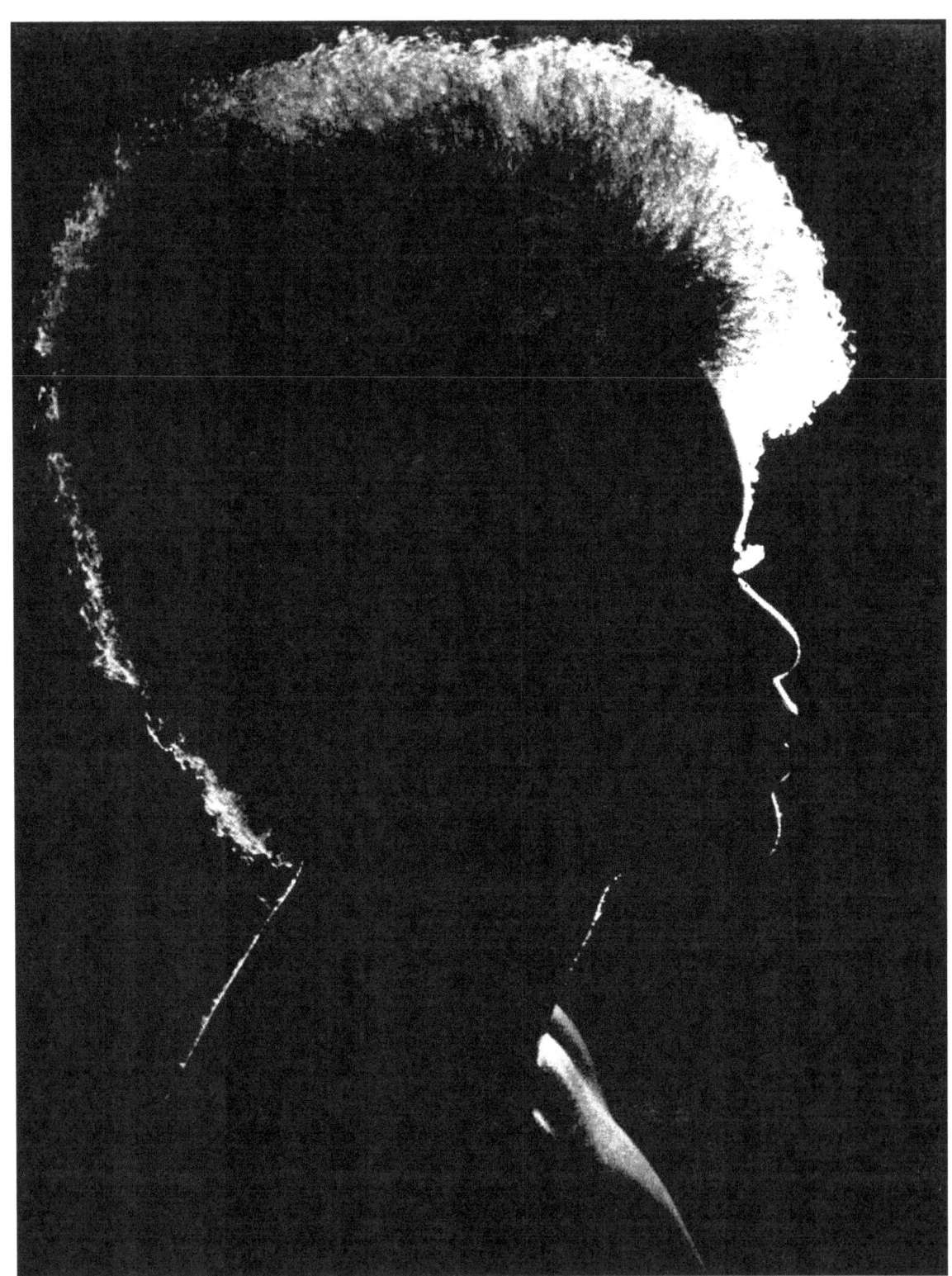

IMPRESSIONS

A BLACK ARTS AND CULTURE MAGAZINE

VOL. 1 NO. 1   DECEMBER, 1974

CONTENTS

6   TIME FOR TRUTH   by Baron James Ashanti
8   SHORT STORY / THE PLAN   by Arthur Flowers
12   HAPPENIN'S / Entertainment Guide
13   FASHION   Designer Rufus Barkley
15   HARRY BELAFONTE SPEAKS AT HARLEM HOSPITAL
24   FRAGMENTS OF A SPIRITUAL   by LeRoy Clarke
     (drawings and poetry)
30   MUSIC / "MEAT ON THE BONE"   by David Jackson
     (profile of Taj Mahal)
32   ESSAY / BLACK ART AND WHITE CRITICS   by Calvin Wilson
34   DANCE / MOVIN'   by Pat Glenn
     (interview with Dianne McIntyre-Choreographer of
     the SOUNDS IN MOTION dance company)
44   NUTRITION / NUTRITIONAL WELL-BEING   by Brenda Bailey
47   THEATER / LIFELINES   by Calvin Wilson

POETRY

4   MARKET WOMAN   by Mervyn Taylor
4   BLOODSTONE   by Baron James Ashanti
43   (untitled)   by Damany-Kenya Tyson
50   BUT IT COMES OUT MAD   by Camille Yarbrough
54   CITY OF CAPITAL   by Baron James Ashanti
55   (untitled)   by Phillis Lu Simpson

PHOTOGRAPHY

2   Bob Bryan
5   Mel Wright
13   Mel Wright
14   Bob Ellison
42   Desmond Smith
46   Mel Wright
52   Lloyd DeSuze
53   Desmond Smith
     Cover Art by LeRoy Clarke

Publisher
Robert Bryan

Art Staff
Herb Henry / Art Director
Nancy Mildren

Literary Editor
Baron James Ashanti

Editors
Pat Glenn / Dance Reviewer
David Jackson / Music Reviewer
Calvin Wilson / Theater Reviewer
Brenda Bailey / Nutrition

MARKET WOMAN

very wide
and tough under the brim
of a faded flower hat
she is fed up with their smiles
their picture-taking
in front of her stall
next time they ask
she will bend over
and show them
her giant sapodillas

mervyn taylor

BLOODSTONE

Everytime I   red spiral   the clamor of the
make love I   shadows   flies of a dollar
feel   teeth   whirlwind
in the cracks   chewing   festering
of my skin   through to   on the eyes of my
                           light &   unborn children;

the sperm disintergrates in her womb
a rifle emerges, baptized by the
                     blood
of a dying fetus, in disobedience I
dismount in search of vengence

Baron James Ashanti
September 27, 1974

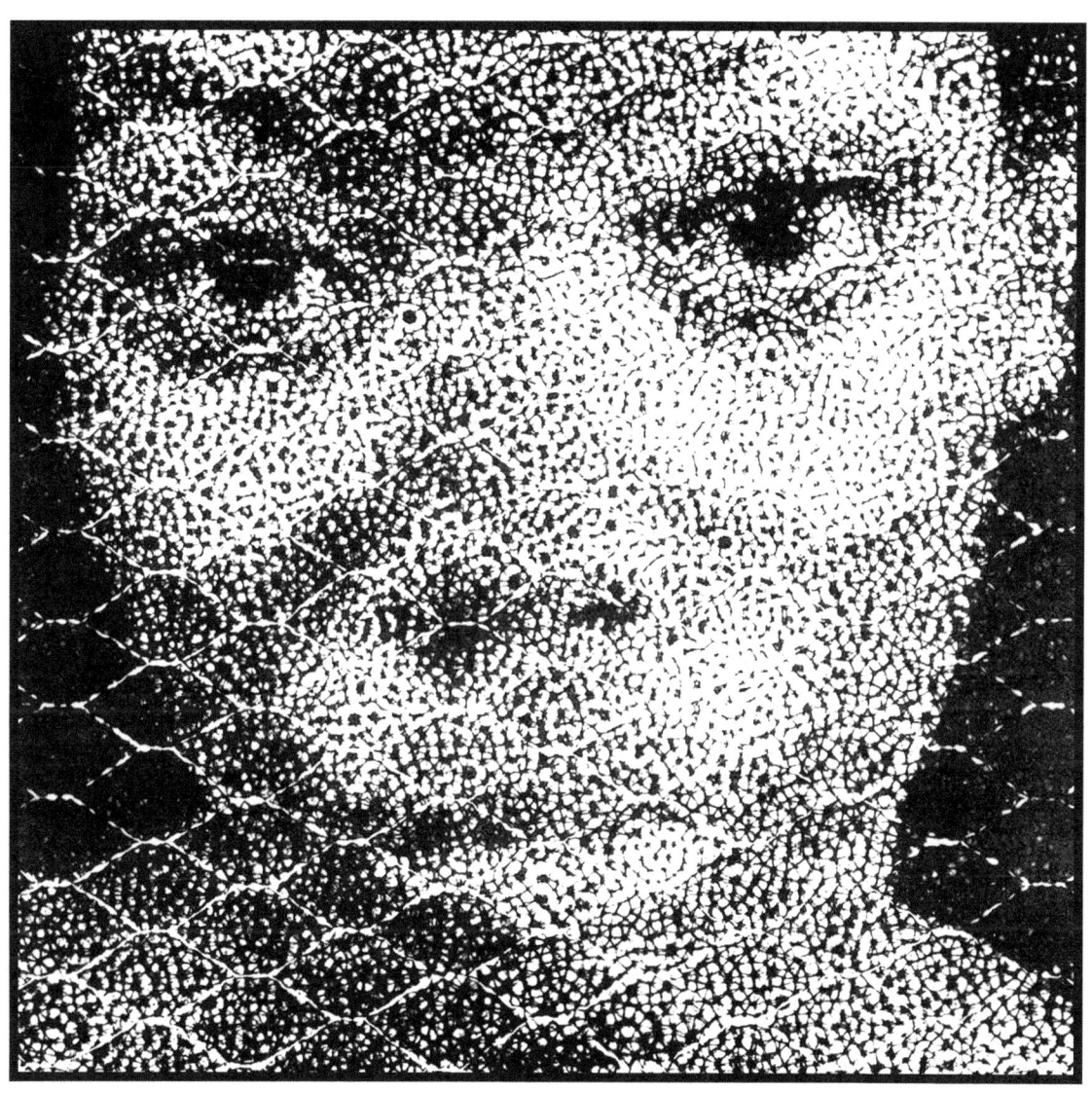

TIME FOR TRUTH

A Message From The Literary Editor

Baron James Ashanti

Nothing is absolute. The universe being in a constant state of constant flux necessitates that everything and everyone who is in harmony with it also be in a state of constant change. As that relates to Black poetry as an art form, I believe that a poet must live, eat, sleep, make love to, and believe in his or her work. A Black poet cannot cry out for struggle, revolutions etc, and then put his/herself on a pedestal above the people. A Black Poet is a people's artist, therefore his/her art is art for people's sake and not the decadent art for arts' sake. There must be a fusion of form and content. I've made this statement because as Blacks, we oft-times forget that we are still as a people trying to survive in amerika, and as such our art forms must be geared towards survival. This must sound cliche, but it still needs to be said.

Having written poetry for fifteen years, I feel that one of the responsibilities of the poet is to grow in discipline, technique, values, visions and principles. If a poet puts out five books and sees no logical progression in form and content, then the relevancy of those books has to be re-examined. No true poet ever sees the same thing in the same light twice. No love is ever like the one before or after. A true poet must succumb to the vision of wandering through a cyclone's eye; a view which is not static, or dogmatic. If a Black Poet allows his work to be published, he is responsible for that publication, be it a single poem or a book. It is highly unlikely that either the publisher, or the poet will recall all copies of the work for defects.

For years those who have controlled Black literature have been able to say what exists and what does not exist. A mere wave of the hand from "leading experts" and Larry Neals' BLACK BOOGALOO does not exist. A mere wish and Askia Muhammad Toures' SONGHAI is a figment of a radical poets' muse. The period covering 1969 to 1974 has seen a total of two reviews for those two pioneering works. Literary ostracism does not alter true reality. Brothers Neal and Toure do exist, their works exist, and they both are fine poets in their own rights. For some reason the oft-times self appointed "Black Literati" feels that if a particular work expressed in poetry threatens their own narrow views it should never have been written. An exclusion from an important anthology dictates who was involved in the creation and inner workings of the fine guerilla publications: SOULBOOK, BLACK DIALOGUE, UMBRA, and the JOURNAL of BLACK POETRY, in the early sixties are pushed aside; and those who have come afterwards are projected as having created the new wave in Black Poetry. For years those who have

controlled Black Literature have played this historical rearranging game.
It's about time the game ended, because
it is not in the best interest of
Black People.

All fruit does not have to be
oranges. There are many levels to
Black poetry. To name a few there
are: lyrical, metaphorical, prosaic,
epic prosaic, afro-surrealism, rap/
street, classical, and narrative.
Any one style should not be a dominate
trend, we need as many levels in pro-
jection as we can muster. All poems
are not masterpieces,however; all
poems should be historical documents.
I mean by this that the poet must
have an eye on what his or her work
will mean to Black generations 25
years from now. As a practicing poet
I feel that poetry for Blacks cannot afford to be "just another
hustle," or just another "get over."
Fame and fortune does not make one
a poet. One is known by ones deeds,
if one writes trash, then one is a
literary tramp; (at the risk of caus-
ing a semantical subterfuge) everything written does need to be published.

I reiterate, one is known by
one's deed's. If you live poetry,
then you are a poet. One cannot
delegate to one's self the distinction
of being a poet in the true sense.
There are Black Poets all over
amerika who will never be published.
There are grandmothers who have been
practicing oral poets all their lives,
and they will never have a thing
published. There are Black common
laborers digging ditches who write
poetry everytime they swing a pick-axe.
The shame about this is that while
everyone is playing follow"the leader"
some white boy will collect something
like "the oral tradition in amerika."
Don't laugh, that's what happened in
the sixties when a certain Mr.KAUGHMAN
went south and ripped off the Black
muse exhibited in work songs etc. He
became a big anti-war folk singing
for his efforts.

As literary editor, I will be
looking for those poets who have not
been able to have anything published;
those who are little heard of because
they do not have access to other magazines because of either the political (progressive) and or experimental
content of their poetry. I believe in
Black People and I believe in Black
People's poetry. I do not think that
poetry in paticular, or culture in
general should be used to rip the
people off for material gains. My
affiliation with IMPRESSIONS MAGAZINE
is based on my belief that it can be a
valid voice of Black culture. I do not
wish to be part of anything which claims
exclusive right to the word. I will
make mistakes in my discharge of my
duties as literary editor, indeed the
magazine itself will make mistakes, but
I'm confident that the magazine will
grow as a useful extention of Black
Culture. At this point I'd like to
declare solidarity with brother Dingane
(Joe Goncalves), Chief Editor of the
Journal of Black Poetry, San Fran-
cisco; a brother who champions the
voice of Black Peoples strength and
urge a progressive direction in culture
and politics; two mainstays in Black
survival.

Yours in the eye of
the cyclone.

"THE PLAN"

BY ARTHUR FLOWERS

It's long past due that Black Folk knew how they'd been tricked by the Lord and the Devil. Now, the Lord and the Devil grew up in the projects, right next door to each other. As young fellas they were always tryin' to outdo each other with tricks. Now the Lord's conversation was much smoother than the Devil's, so round about early 20th century- here it was Holy War IV - and the Devil ain't won but one (partying, like you never seen after the flood; Devil racked up).

Devil 'cided to call a meetin' of the board, get his best minds together to do something about the soul problem. At the time, the Lord was pullin' eight souls to each two by the Devil. Devil couldn't understand it. After all, he was offering the good life, food for body and mind, beaucoup party, good music, and plenty room for advancement. All Heaven offered was callouses on the knees and a jive two week paid vacation.

After the minutes had been read, the Devil told the forty assembled Arch Demons of the Board that,if somethin' wasn't done right soon, they'd all have to resign and start again at the bottom. Since the Arch Demons of the Board felt the pit beneath them, many plenty potent ideas were expoused. For 300 days and 300 nights they labored mightily and all over the earth there was love among man for the Devil was not about his business.

Then, on the 301st day, one of the winged lesser Demons- who worked a side show on his off days- came before the actin' Sergeant At Arms, Old Man Beezlebub (the Devil's main man and Captain in Chief of the Armed Forces) with a request to speak to the Devil.

The Devil was tired, still cool, but he was tired. Six of the Arch Demons of the Board had died of exhaustion and still they hadn't come up with no action. Seems that the Lord's Public Relations People were just too tough, and his Indoctrination and Propaganda Branch was the envy of any halfway self-respectin' leader. So be it known that the Devil and the Board were open to suggestion. The lesser demon was brought before the white porcelain throne of the Devil. He fluttered his left wing nervously; he had never seen the Chief in person before.

"Well,Chief," he started, "It's like this,'member back to when you won THE BATTLE OF THE GARDEN?"

At the mention of THE BATTLE OF THE GARDEN, the assembled Demons began to shout and cheer lustily, raisin' their wine bottles in a toast to the Chief.

"Yeah Chief, that was smooth!"

"Didn't Chief pull that off smoother'n a mutha?"

"Ol' Chief was tough then wudn't he?"

"Hell man, Chief's still tough!"

The assembled Demons got ecstatic and began to lose their cool.
Soon, they were hoppin', runnin', crawlin', prancin', and flyin' all over
the meetin' hall. The Devil calmly snuffed his joint with the tip of his
tail, nodded to Captain Bee, and order was soon restored. The Devil turned to the lesser Demon.
"Continue."
"'Member how you handled that? Those two had already signed with
that other outfit. But you got 'em to break their contract 'cause you
dangled that apple in front of their eyes and they had been told that it
wasn't for 'em. Knowing those animals like you did, you knew that if you
tell 'em 'sumpin' ain't for em then that's what they want. So, "Heaven
Forbid," eh eh -a little humor there Chief,- uh hmmph...you dangled that
apple for nothing down and forever to pay. Then you whealt and you dealt
and you led 'em to the joys of righteous sinnin'."
"Chief dealt alright," wailed one of the greater demons. "He dealt
on their ass!"
"Brought limin' scunion didn't he?"
"Sho' did!"
"Yeah, Chief sure figured them creatures right!"
"That Lord fella blew, when he picked that one! Been betta off pick-
ing a cat."
"Mo intelligent anyway!"

Once again, the demons were runnin' wild; the huge meetin' hall
quivered and shook. The Chief lanquidly extended his diamond ringed pinky
and a burst of blue flame shot to the ceiling, sizzlin' and a cracklin',
blisterin' and a burnin'. The Demons cowered in their seats, starin' at
the Chief and mutterin' foul damnable curses. Not out loud though, 'cause
the Chief hadn't flamed up like that since '32 when the price of brimestone
rose to the heavens. The Devil turned to the lesser demon.
"Continue." The Devil, he cool as ever.
"Anyhoo Chief, here's my idea. We make a symbolic thing you know?
Have it represent fame 'n fortune!"

From the amen corner, like an overeager echo,"Fame 'n fortune!"
"Love!" screamed the winged one,"Beauty, happ'ness, sucess, riches,
Dreams Deferred! We ration it, only to a few,'n we tell everybody
else that they can't afford it; it ain't theirs to have, it is not
to be!"
Group: "Amen brother, be mean!"
"No slack, no mercy!"

The little Devil took a long stride. His voice took on deep melod-
ious tones and in a bass singsong he ran it down.
"Better yet, get 'em deep in debt!"

A low soulful moan came from the assembled Demons and one of the
most revered, plank backed, no slacked, dressed black,Arch Demons of the
Board, laid on with a mighty, "MMmmmm Mmmmyeah!"

The little Demon cut loose with a powerful groan, "Wooaaoohh
can you see it Chief? Aaww gon' be good. Some envy, a little greed,
a lotta hate, pretentionin', false Goddin', covetin' 'n doin' 'n
dealin', all the truely great sins. Oooh, can you see it,Chief?"

His voice roared. It rose and dipped and took the Demons along for the ride as he stode back and forth in front of the white porcelain throne of the Devil. Around the strategy table furry heads were rhythmically bobbin'. Even the Devil lay back with his eyes closed and a big shiteatin' grin on his face. His tail twitched and his hooves kept the beat. Like he was seein' it.

The winged one was off into it, damn near screamin', it was my man's finest hour. The little Devil was so hot, that sweat on his forehead started steamin'. The meetin' hall was filled with the smell of sulphur 'cause my man was smokin'. And the Amens were comin' solid and strong. The little devil say,

"Alotta pain, alotta misery, and they finally got it. We send in a special squad to tear it up! Put 'em even deeper in the hole and closer to the pit! Frustration Chief, can you see the frustration? Murder, suicide, self mutilation, wife beatin', child beatin', Chief I can't stand it; it's so good to me. Death, doom and destruction to 'em. Star action,Chief, can you sseee it?!"
" I see it, I see it!" yelled one of the greater Demons. "Goddamn if I don't see it!"
"She sound good to me,Chief!"
"I bet we even catch some of them lowlifeted preacher fellas."
"I think the brother got a winner."
"Damned if he ain't!"

The Demons were tearin' up the place. Somebody turned on the sounds, Low Lip Eddie pulled out his drums, and the Demons started gettin' down. Plaster fell from the ceilin' and the floor took a beatin'. The din was unnervin', a most unholy racket, cawin', snarlin', laughin', spittin', crackin', cacklin', and some young diddybob turned the volume up on the box. The strange thing about it was that these dudes were usually cool. I talkin' 'bout they don't come no cooler than the Arch Demons of the Board.

But then you knew they were cool,'cause the soft click of Cap'n Bee releasin' the safety off his big magnum brought immediate quiet. So quiet they heard a rat under the table fart and mumble"Scuse me man." The demons tried to look casual and inconspicuous as they scuttled back to their seats. For in The Valley of The Shadow of Death, Meetin' Hall #2, Cap'n Bee was known to be a terrible old pistol-totin' fool.

Now the Devil, he so cool, he ain't even not moved. He still laid back on the throne, eyes closed. After an hour or so, he stood and said,
"I like it, do I hear a motion?"
"Motion!"
"Second!"
"All in favor?" asked the Devil.
A chorus of "AYE'S".
"ALL opposed?"
One demon stood, Bro Showboat from the South Side. Sharp, always clean. He stands and says.
"Chief, the brothers action is mighty fine,

I can see all those great sins a multiplyin'
And the list is impressive, true enough a fact,
But, doin' 'n dealin'? What in the hell is that?"

The Devil say "Hhmmm?" He turns to the lesser Demon,"I'm familiar
with your other sins and great they be, but what in the hell is Doin' 'n
Dealin'?"

"Well Chief," says the winged one, "I was referrin' to the Third
Tablet."

"The third tablet?"

"Right Chief, you know, the ones with the Thou Shalts and the Thou
Shalt Nots The Third Tablet!"

"Oh, that tablet!" says the Devil, "The one that had Commandments
Eleven through Fifteen? Always wondered what happened to that last
five. How did they go? Uh, sumpin' 'bout, uh, Thou Shalt Not Dope
Thy Brother's Mind, and sumpin' like, uh, Thou Shalt Not Sell Thy
Mother's Body, and sumpin' like, uh, lemme see now, uh oh yeah,
one 'bout whoppin' Thy Brother's Head, and that sho' nuff powerful
one 'bout Respectin' Thy Sister, and uh, shit!. Those were the best
ones, some damned good material. We'da got some good play outta
those. What in the hell did happen to 'em?"

The little Demon says, "Well Chief, my granddaddy was there and he
told it to me like this. You 'member that General they had on that
front, the long haired one?"

"You must be talkin' 'bout Moses, the one with the light jones?"

"Light jones my ass! Chief, dude was a junkie you unnastan! And
he didn't wanna come up off that dope noway, and since those stone
tablet were heavy, and he didn't have but two arms, he just left
that third one on top of that mountain!"

"Well I be damned!" says the Devil. "And those were the good ones.
Left 'em huh?" Why is it that the Almighty Farce didn't smite him?"

"Well he wudn't interested too tough in those noway Chief. They
didn't have nothin' to do with procedure. He figured that if he
hung the people up in bullshit, that their minds would be too tired
to deal with Realities. Tellin' 'em 'bout how to treat each other
ain't got nothin' to do with heaven and hell and he was scared you
and him would have to go back to a nine to five." The Devil shudd-
ered.

Devil lay back and muses on the winged ones plan. He mutters to
himself, "Hhmm, a symbolic thing you say? Dreams Deferred. Ration
it, only a few, frustration." The Devil pops his fingers. Snap
"Deeper in the hole..." Snap " and closer to the pit! Yeah, I like
that. So be it! That five kinda dangerous but if we slick enough
they'll never know. Cap'n Bee I wantchu to get a committee together
on that right away and I want a report on my desk in the morning!"

With that the Devil buttoned his vest, threw his coat over his should-
er and got up to leave the meetin' hall. One of the Arch Demons of
the Board, representin' the lower regions, stood and stopped him,

"Chief, what'll we call it?"

The devil turned to the lesser Demon, who worked that side show on
his off days, "It's your baby, give it a codename!"
"Well Chief, uh, CADILLAC sounds kinda good to me."

AND SO IT CAME TO PASS THAT THE DEVIL DOIN" MUCH BETTER

HAPPENIN'S

HARLEM CULTURAL CENTER
137th ST. & 7th Avenue
245-8125/523-5199

Dec. 4	VINIE BURROWS *	
5	ROGER FURMAN *	SYMBOLS: * 7:30 PERFORMANCES
6	WEUSI KUUMBA TROUPE *	** MATINEE(2:30)PERF.
7	JU JU PLAYERS ***	*** MAT. & EVENING PERF.
8	BED-STUY THEATER, INC *	

$3.00 or TDF VOUCHERS

URBAN ARTS CORPS THEATER
26 WEST 20th STREET
724-7820

PLAYING NOW   "UPS AND DOWNS OF THEOPHILUS MAITLAND"

 THURS, FRI,& SAT-7:30 SUN 3:00 $2.50 or TDF VOUCHER
LYRICS BY MICKI GRANT-BOOK BY VINNETTE CARROLL

NEW HERITAGE REPERTORY THEATER
43 WEST 125th STREET
876-3272

NOW PLAYING   "STRIVERS ROW"   DONATION: $3.00 or TDF VOUCHER
SATIRE BY ABRAM HILL   DIRECTED BY ROGER FURMAN   FRI. & SAT. 8:00   SUN. 3:00

BILLIE HOLIDAY THEATER
1368 FULTON STREET   (corner of Marcy Ave)
636-0919/8

DEC. 6&7	"THE AMEN CORNER"	BY JAMES BALDWIN	$3.50	8PM
8	"	"	"	3PM
13&14	"SISTER SON/JI"	SONIA SANCHEZ	"	8PM
15	THE EAST RIVER PLAYERS PRESENTS "PREMA...ON A SERIOUS NOTE"			
	(A MUSICAL EVENING)		$3.50	3PM
20&21	"STREET SOUNDS"	BY ED BULLINS	"	8PM
22	THE EAST RIVER PLAYERS PRESENTS MS. MARY CHAPMAN, SONG STYLIST			
	(AN EVENING OF FASHION & SONG)		$3.50	8PM

******
DEC 19   DR. YOSEF BEN JOCHAMAN: LECTURE AND DISCUSSION "AFRICA'S
            CONTRIBUTION TO THE WORLD."   FREE

              "THE PRODIGAL SISTER"   WRITTEN BY J.E.FRANKLIN

PRESENTED AT: THEATER DELYS   BOX OFFICE OPENS AT NOON
                121 CHRISTOPHER STREET
                WA4-8782   SHOWS: TUES-FRI 8PM
                                                     SAT 6:30&10:00
                                                     SUN 3:PM & 7PM

con't on page 60

RUFUS BARKLEY

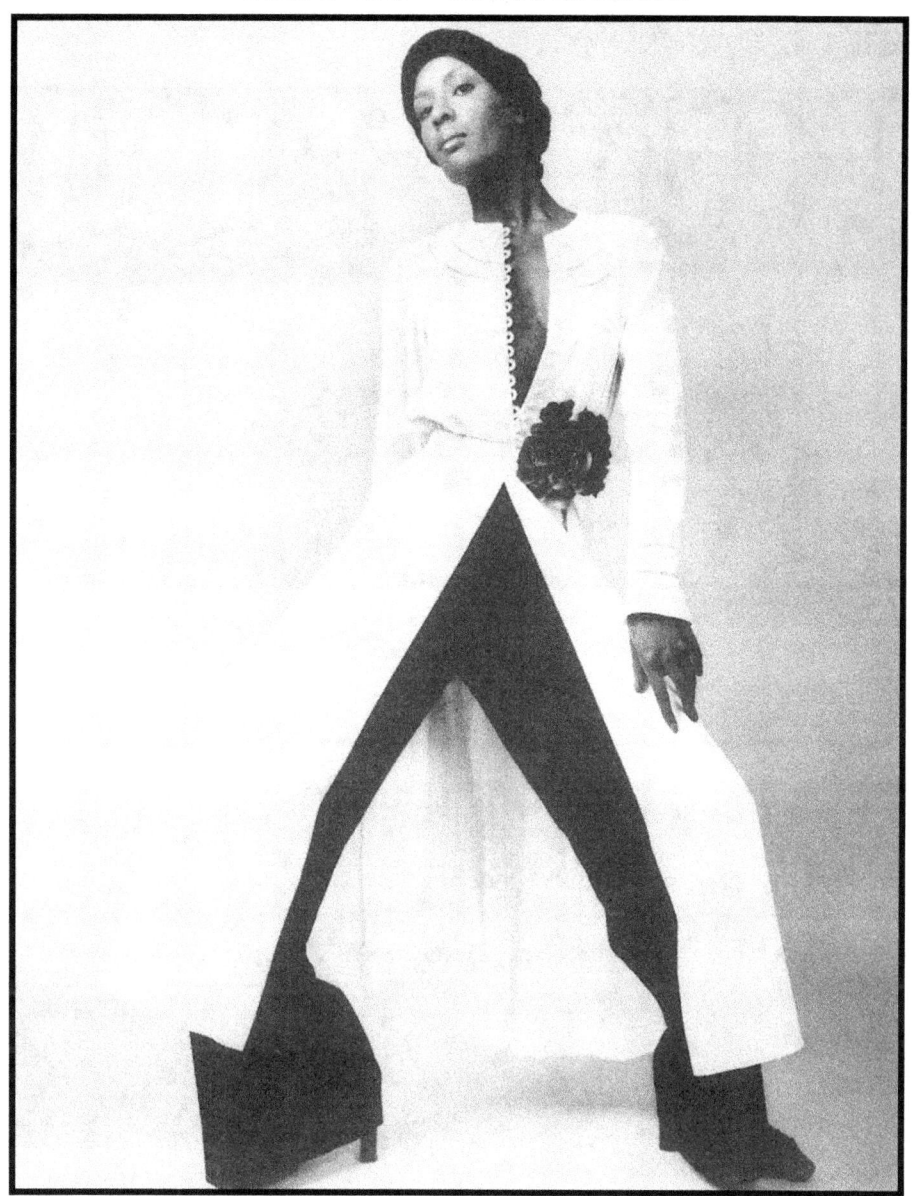

Modeled by Juanita Hewlett

Designer Rufus Barkley, born and raised in Harlem has come a long way on his journey to the top. Consistent in the quality of his creations, Rufus has designed for many years with the Ebony Fashion Fair and is now savoring his success as a full time designer on Seventh Avenue.

"In designing, I believe in doing a day into evening concept. With the strong influence of sportswear in the industry today, separates play a very important part." Introducing his new creation, Rufus comments "The black crepe pants can be removed from under the white dress top. Then you would have a white crepe mid-calf or mid-length dress."

Rufus is definitely a designers designer who sees Black Fashion,"as a mood and an attitude set by the young Black girl, and refined by the Black woman." With his obvious talents and sensitivity, Rufus is a designer that has for years been in tune with the Black Woman and understands her changing tastes well. Interested sisters who desire to acquire the above creation should definitely call or write to IMPRESSIONS for more information. We, at IMPRESSIONS wish to express our gratitude to Rufus for his kindness in sharing his talent with us and wish him the best.

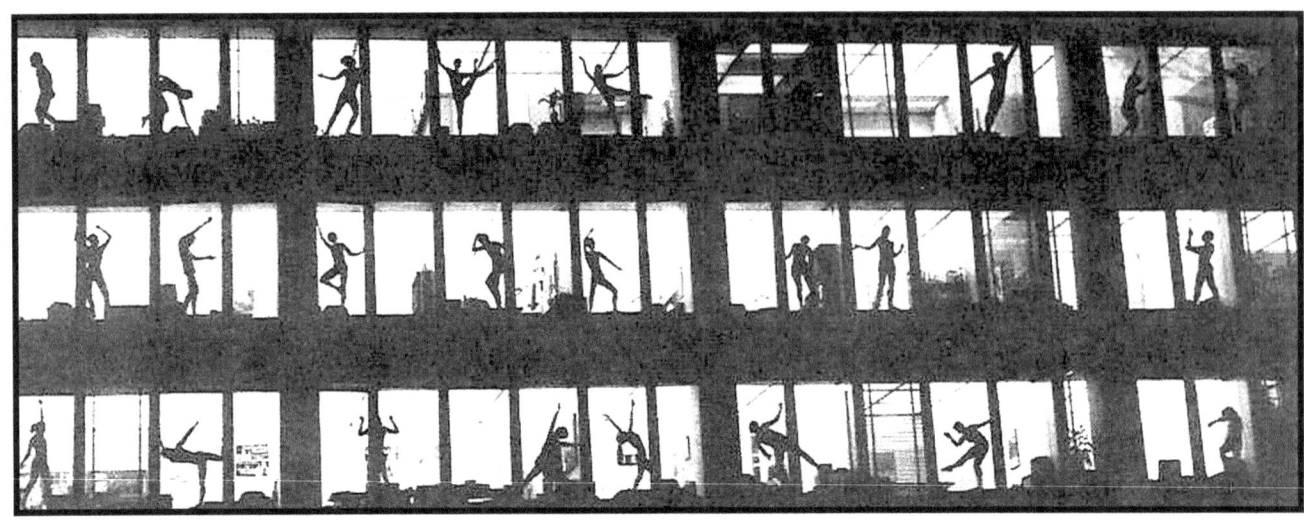

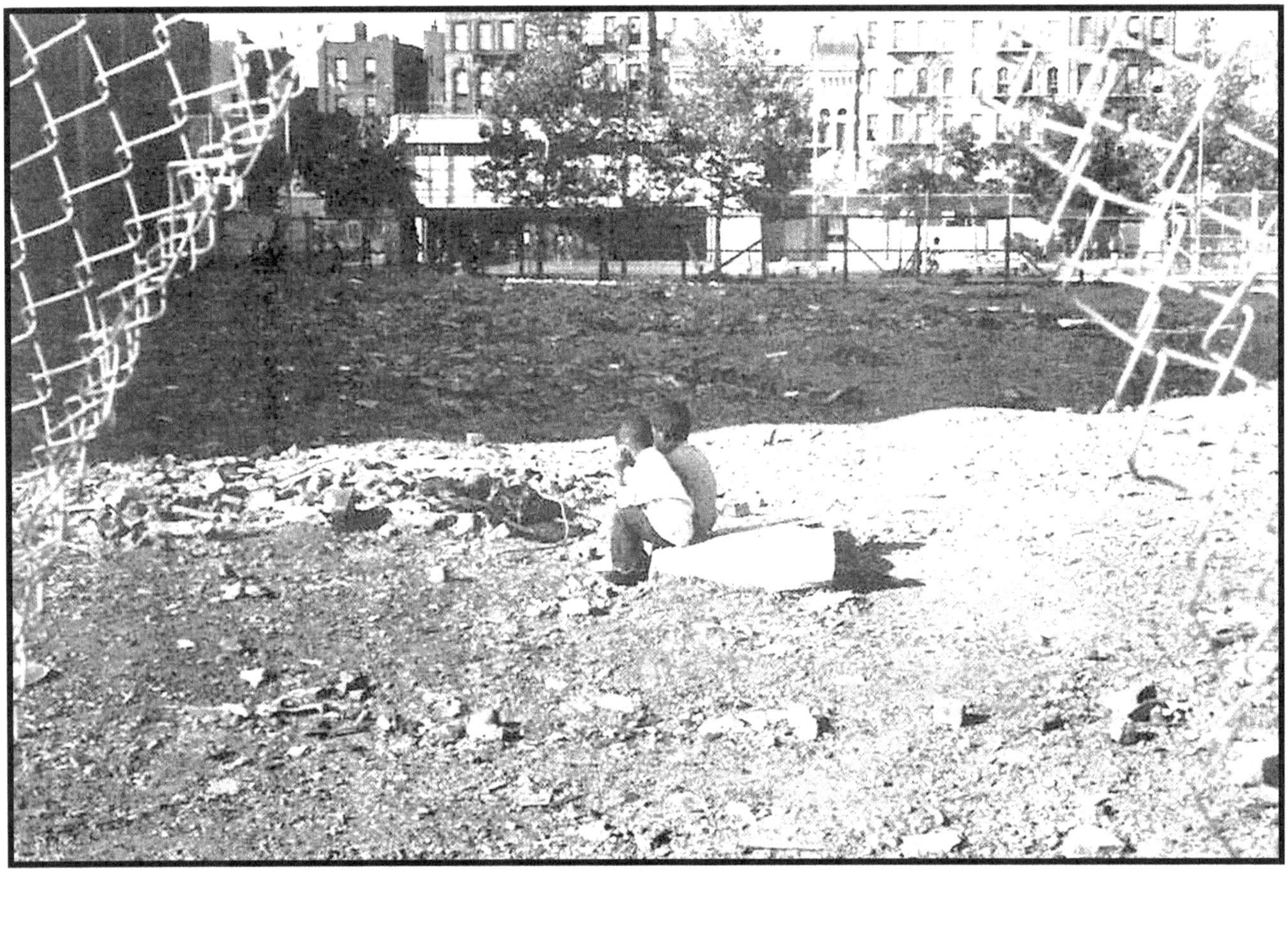

HARRY BELAFONTE
Speaks At Harlem Hospital

I eagerly look forward to being able to come here this afternoon, for several reasons. I think the most important one is that I am a product of the Harlem community. I was born on 141st street and 7th avenue (2460 7th avenue). At the age of five-that would be around 1932-I was hit by a car on 7th avenue. I spent alot of time in this hospital trying to recupe from those injuries as a little boy. I laid unconscious for about - I don't know-for about 2 days, I was told - and from my many experiences in this community I have come a long way in life.

I haven't come a long way in life just because I possess very special qualities,'cause if that were the only prerequisite, I think that many people who have not come a long way in life, should have, in fact, come a long way in life. I've come a long way in life through a series of coincidences that took place in my life giving me the type of platform where I was able to full-fill the kinds of dreams that I had in my adolescence. Most young people are able to dream from the time that they approach their formative years. I've found that being black, being born in Harlem, that there were very few things in the 1930's that I could really aspire to, because an extremely harsh society left dreams for black folks a thing that was very elusive, something that couldn't be fullfilled.

DREAMS DEFERRED. Couldn't be fullfilled because you were not only the pawns of a society that was objectly cruel, but because we as a people, in the mist of that cruelty had been denied so much knowledge about who and what we were. I didn't know that there was a FREDERICK DOUGLASS; I didn't know that there was a DR.DUBOIS; I didn't know that there was a NAT TURNER and a SOJOURNER TRUTH, cause in the schools that I went to in Harlem, none of these things were taught to me.

As I grew up in this community-my father, who was a seaman,who worked very hard in the ranks of organized labor to try to get the Maritime Unions organized so that sailors-Black sailors-he was a West Indian-could get work, to become part of the major force in commerce of this nation. I saw him come home many a night, bloody from the kind of fights and the kinds of things that took place in the union halls when blacks were trying to involve themselves deeply in the ranks of labor. My mother was a domestic worker and she got part-time work from white folks downtown and between my father's trips away, which would be for months at a time and my mothers deep involvement with trying to make the family survive; she had to abandon us like most mothers had to abandon their children even today in order to pursue those things, to make the family cohesive. So, on one of those nights, I was out playing in the streets when I shouldn't have been but when you're five, it's very hard to tell you what you should or shouldn't have been doing. You've just don't have that kind of perceptiveness; you do what's good for you-what feels good and runnin' the streets for me, felt good. 'Specially when there was nobody around to tell me what I could not do or tell me where I shouldn't be.

After that experience, my mother then moved my brother and I down to the West Indies. Of course, although she and all of her family worked on the plantations that were owned by white folks, there was one essential benefit of being down in the West Indies, in that, there wasn't a whole lot of cars.

The cruelty of colonialism is not to be denied but the essence of it is qualitatively different from the kinds of conditions that we face here as Blacks in America. So, for a good portion of my life, I was left to roam the hills and to roam the streets moving from family to family and I grew up with a culture that was later on able to become the root of much that I was to call upon as an artist.

RETURN TO AMERICA. When I came back to the U.S. in the late 30's, I went to school. I lived on Manhattan Avenue and I lived on Amsterdam Avenue and I lived on 130th Street and we moved from place to place because that was one way you could duck the rent (laughter). Yeah, 'cause we had to do that too. We tried damned hard to pay it, because my family is a family of dignity; they weren't looking to get away with anything. But, if you just didn't have it....? For the first month we used to stay very quiet on those days that we thought the landlord was going to come by; nobody inside would say anything. Then we'd breathe again because we knew that he didn't live in the community-he was an absentee landlord. He wouldn't be back until a month later and if you could get away for 2 months, you were lucky. So, once in a while my mother would change the name and move on to another community, but those weren't things of dishonor; those were instruments of survival.

When I went to George Washington H.S. I found that going to school every day was a...a...very, very hard experience. Alot of us as young boys belonged to gangs in the neighborhood. Little gangs called the Buckaneers, the Midtown Midgets; little gangs called the Scorpions and we constantly raided one another, and if there was a rip-off that took place that one gang wanted to avenge, they would wait for you until you got out of school and nab you. I always seemed to have the knack of being in the wrong gang and the wrong place at the wrong time.

So, going to high school became, and I'm making it as brief as possible-I could go into great detail about other things-going to school became a very difficult experience. I was preoccupied with survival; I was preoccupied with where my father was; I was preoccupied with wondering what my mother had to do; I was preoccupied with wondering with those things which made me feel the responsibility of having to take care of my brother and a few cousins who were running around. So, by the time I was 16½, I had optioned to change my geographical location. I decided that if I could seduce my mother into joining me in lying about my age, I could maybe, enter the U.S. Navy and in that time I'd be able to go off and see a bit of the world and learn a little bit more about life than I was capable of learning, let loose in the streets of Harlem. Well, we couldn't pull that one off. So I had to wait until I was 17 and when I was 17, I enlisted.

U.S. NAVY. I joined the U.S. Navy and that's kind of ironic in a way because the Navy was a very important experience in my life. I have since grown to be a man who is adamently opposed to the military: adamently opposed to war, adamently opposed to be a part of any force that is principally used to suppress peoples of colour in most of the areas of the world (applause)...but what the U.S. Navy did do for me-in those days the armed forces was segregated; you were all Black men in Black units. Young men, old men, middle aged men but men nevertheless. And in those days, I was for the first time thrown into the center of men, who possessed intellectual qualities; who possessed some intellectual background-because in our unit we had men who came from college; we had men who were doctors; we had men who were lawyers and that was quite astounding to me because I didn't know that we had Black lawyers and Black people who possessed academia that gave them the platform of expertise. Even when I came to Harlem Hospital in those days, the handful of doctors who were here-the very few of them were

Black, most of them were white-but what happened to me in the Navy was that I began to hear names like FREDERICK DOUGLAS and I began to hear names like W.E.B. DUBOIS and I became aware of a man by the name of PAUL ROBESON and I heard for the first time about the NAACP and these things hit upon a barren land of emotion that was ready for bringing forth a land of plenty and my brothers in the armed services helped water that barren land and it began to bear fruit.

Although I had great difficulty reading; although I saw no future in going to school at the time; they made me understand that knowledge was a very precious thing. So I went out on my own and I began to read and I began to know and I began to ask questions for the first time. With all the anger that I've had as a boy in Harlem, I now began to channel. I became somewhat irascible; I became defiant. I became defiant against those men who stood in command of my battalion. When, I began to ask,"Why they are segregated?" I was given all kinds of explanations that weren't satisfactory. It wasn't so much that I wanted to live with white folks, as a matter a fact, I didn't. But I wanted the option to be able to go where I wanted and to go and do what I wanted to do but those options were continually denied me. Instead of feeling a sense of futility I seized upon this knowledge and when I came out of the U.S. NAVY after almost two years; I decided to seek out these men and these women that I've heard about.

So, I discovered where PAUL ROBESON was and I went to meet with him and I found out that DR. DUBOIS was living in Brooklyn and I went with him and that became a very important part of my life because these were the men with whom I studied and they were able to give me profound truth and profound guidance in what I was ultimately going to do with my life.

When I choose to become an artist; I choose to become an artist because I saw the opportunity to be able to use that platform to express those things which were passionate and meaningful to Black People, not only in America but Black People in the West Indies and all over the world. My success as an artist wasn't something that I set out to do because in those days that I came along, that success at best represented great limitations. But, I pursued it nevertheless because I wanted to express myself and I would not permit anyone to deny me that platform. I must say, when I came out of the Navy, I'll never forget that when I told my mother that I had decided to use the G.I. bill of rights-that subsidy which gave us the opportunity to go to school as a veteran- and I told her that I was going to study to be an actor, to be a dramatist; she went into a great decline. She at least felt that after having had the kind of background that I did, at least I would be able to use that opportunity to become a Doctor, a Lawyer, an Accountant - and I had a GOOD head for figures. I had to, because what I didn't tell you was that when I was a small boy, I was also a numbers runner (laughter). Well yes, I was, but that's not being solicitous by saying that; it's a fact.

My family was West Indian and West Indians had a very powerful position in this community. They just didn't know how to tolerate certain things and if they found it impossible to live within the law; they decided to survive outside of it, (applause) and collecting numbers was one of the best ways. As a matter of fact it meant that every Saturday I could go on down to my uncle Neddies house and there was always $10.00 waiting 'cause if he had a good week and nobody had any heavy hits, he could spread it around a little bit. So I used to take that $10.00 and go out and that fed us for the week and my mother knew more of what to do with a chicken than a chicken knew what to do with itself (laugh).

So, I have a good head for figures but out of desire...I don't know what it was, I don't know why...it just happened. I wanted to be an artist-because

ROBESON meant profoundly so much to me and when I began to meet people like CANADA LEE; when I began to hear about people like CATHRINE DUNHAM, then I began to meet these people and the more I met them, the more I saw their power. Power, that was used in an admirable way. People don't understand that I had a calling and that I should at least pursue that calling to try to make the best of it and in the pursuit of it. If I'd fail, I'd fail on my own and if I were to succeed, I'd succeed on my own. But there was an incident that took place that made my popularity grow beyond my wildest imagination and it grew primarily in the camp of white people.

CIVIL RIGHTS MOVEMENT. It was very hard to work in Harlem getting the kind of money I used to get. I played the Apollo Theatre a couple of times and then when I'd moved out of that enviornment and moved into a broader set of community affairs; I found that it was impossible for me to come back to Harlem-the seat of my life that meant so much and the center of my life that had meant so much and the center of my life that had meant so much and to extract from the communities the monies that I had become accustomed to earning. So, I'd decided that I would not work in Harlem for profit and alot of people up here have never seen me in this community in a place of commercial endeavor. But I'm sure if some of you would seek out a few of the churches that I have sung at and seek out a few of the places that I have been in behalf of Black causes. If you go out to Rikers Island, where I have visited and sung for the prisoners, you would know that I have been deeply involved in the Black community, in my own Harlem. But, I wasn't running for political office, so there was no need to publicize it. I don't really care whether anybody approves of me or not. As long as, I know that as a man, I have fullfilled what I considered to be a life filled with dignity and integrity and that I'm doing the best that I can to meet the needs of the day and the struggle for liberation. So I did that for awhile and then, when the platform began to broaden and my success became even more intense; I decided to use all of that and to throw it deeply into the heart of what was ultimately to be called the CIVIL RIGHTS MOVEMENT.

I was involved long before that. I was involved in the 40's and in the 50's. I was gathered with a handful of Black People who were viciously under the attack by the United States government, by an instrument called McCARTHYISM. You hear much about what happened to white people under that terrible era, but very few people people know what happened to Black folks under that terrible era. Some of you may remember what happened to PAUL ROBESON under McCARTHYISM, but not many of you know about what happened to the rest of us. But we survived it and in my survival I became deeply involved in the CIVIL RIGHTS MOVEMENT and that took me into two (2) major centers of involvement. One was as an adviser and as a worker in the SOUTHERN CHRISTIAN LEADERSHIP CONFERENCE and in my deep and close association with MARTIN LUTHER KING JR. and then my involvement with the STUDENT NON-VIOLENT CO-ORDINATING COMMITTEE, which gave me the opportunity to embrace such magnificat young men as: RAP BROWN, STOKELY CARMICHAEL, JULLIAN BOND, JAMES FOREMAN and a host of others. And I stayed with that and I used my platform, whenever I could to raise money for bail, to get us out of jail..to be able to bring visability to the things that we wanted to do, in registering Blacks to vote. And we came to this city, constantly, doing our thing and then I began to watch us in the Black community become polarized..DR. KING was considered to be a hankerchief head. He was considered to be a man who was not intense enough nor volatile enough, nor aggressive enough and many, under the umbrella that DR. KING provided were beginning to move towards what was termed militant or extreme acts. Well, I had to say like LORRAINE HANSBERRY:"If the law is an unjust law, then it must be changed. If, in the process of changing it, you are afraid of its consequences, then you do not belong in the struggle. But if you're not afraid of the consequences, then be prepared to go to jail; be prepared to die even,if you believe profoundly and strongly enough in change; if there's injustice! (applause). So, with that as a guideline, I pursued my work in the CIVIL RIGHTS MOVEMENT. And I watched also in the Black community the polarization take place. There was one one camp and then another camp and then this group and then that group. The thing that became painful to me was that we were more doing it to ourselves, than the white oppressor was doing it to us. We were incapable of coming together with the understanding that we all shared a common destiny and as men and women who suffered under that yolk of oppression, that we belonged to each other and that we should find the real meaning of coalition and move on because all of us function in different ways and have different gifts to bring. It is interesting that when DR. KING was murdered and all those who found him too passive, not aggressive enough not articulate enough in where they wanted it to go, soon had no platform for themselves either. Where are those movements? Where are all those organizations that had the answers? There is no DR. KING now. Now is your time to move! Now you had a clear shot at it! Bring your thing to the fore. But, it couldn't be brought to the fore because we hadn't really taken care of business and hadn't truly done our homework.

That leads me to make this observation: the essential difference in the Harlem today, as I see it and the Harlem that I grew up in is that there is no doubt that ghetto life and all the oppressive things that take place in that life produces a condition that is debasing. If you are treated like an animal long enough, it is almost a fact that you'll have to respond like an animal. But we were able to hang on as a people to a great morality, draw a line on a certain kind of ethical conduct. For instance, if we were in the middle of a rumble and Jimmy Jones was in the opposing gang and we saw Mrs. Jones coming down the street, we cooled it and if she had some packages we would grab them and help her get upstairs. Then we'd get back downstairs and pick up where we left off.

What is the essential difference from the Harlem now, is that there is no more respect for Mrs. Jones. When she walks through the streets, even when there is no rumble taking place with neighborhood gangs, she is liable to walk into her own home and find herself ripped off, sometimes murdered, sometimes mutilated. This hospital is filled with such cases - working women who come home to a hostile enviornment because somewhere along the line that moral fiber which once held us all together began to break down and we seem or we seemed to be incapable of putting those forces together and say,"We draw a line," at least for ourselves, as to what we will or will not do to each other.

So, when I first got my opportunities in Hollywood to become an actor, to perform in the media of motion pictures making, I set as my guideline that I would **never** perform or involve myself in anything that did not encourage the best that was in Black people and project a platform that gave white people an even broader understanding-and there was so much that they did not understand-about us.

TELEVISION AND FILM INDUSTRIES. When I look at television today and see some of my early pictures played back, I listen to my son and some of his friends talk and they don't quite understand what all of the noise was about,

19

just because I'm seen talking to a white person and especially a white woman. "What was so big about that?" He hadn't grown up in a time when that wasn't no longer an issue. When we did that picture ISLAND IN THE SUN, I did it because we were told that there was no way in the world, that Black people and white people EVER could be seen on the screen together doing anything that was going to be viable and meaningful to the motion picture industry. I didn't personally care for the picture. It wasn't what I sought to do as an actor. I didn't even feel my juices in it. But I really felt that it was a tactically important thing to do because we've got to break down the mythy first, in order to plant the kinds of seeds and build the kinds of things that we wanted to build, so I made the movie; it was tactical.

When I did CARMEN JONES, they didn't even use my voice when I was singing; it was dubbed. I made the picture because I felt tactically it was important because there was for a long time a myth running through Hollywood, that anything that was all Black was doomed to failure and they recited one picture after an-other, they gave us: CABIN IN THE SKY, ALL GOD'S CHILDREN GOT WINGS, and a host of others and they always showed you the ledger, they said "Well, that picture never did anything and it's just a cardinal rule that Black People all together in a picture can't make no money; so you've got to find another way." So when this chance came and I saw that I could be associated with DOROTHY DANDRIDGE and PEARL BAILEY and OTTO PREMINGER was the director and HAMMERSTEIN had written the libretto. Twentieth Century Fox's HAROLD ZANER was going to be behind it; I said that I can't be caught out-flanked in this one. We got to be in there 'cause I think it could make it and if it makes it, at least we've given another blow to the myth. So we did the picture and it was an instant success, all over the world.

So, at least two things they couldn't say anymore: they couldn't say that Black people cannot be successful in an all Black thing. They couldn't say that Black folks on the screen with white folks don't make any money. Right on the heels of that came a man who is my cloest friend today, SIDNEY POITER. And he came in at the same time when it was absolutely strategic and with his great beauty, with his great dignity and his great talent, he maintained the posture throughout the course of this life of his. We can all sit here and disagree in subtle form or maybe even in passionate form about what he had done and what he has not done, but at no time did any of us ever charge him with having ever been an enemy of the Black People, as in having approached his work with anything less than dignity.

I take great exception with SIDNEY about alot of the things that he's played, wish he hadn't done it but never because it was without dignity. Only because I thought it was time he use his energy in other ways. There's one thing that's a cardinal rule in Hollywood and that is that the Black Community is the single consistent goer of any ethnic group in the U.S.A. to the motion pictures. I don't care whether it was Tarzan or it was Lassie or it was DORIS DAY in her little mythical white farm somewhere in the mid-west. No matter what it was, we went and we went without consciousness. We went and saw ourselves depicted as shiftless, uninventive, deprived group filled with nothing but dumbness and over-sexuality, and even in our own AFRICA we had to be led by a white man swinging through trees 'cause we didn't know how to do nothing. And we went and supported that and all that was part of what fed into us, but something magnificent happened.

Along with the civil rights movement and all of the things that we learned from that, Black People began to have a new consciousness about themselves. They began to have a little consciousness about their heritage. They began to think in terms of what are we and where are we going and with this consciousness? It

20

became very visible that all of a sudden, Black people weren't going to the movies
no more. They were serving white people with a very heavy notice, that until
you begin to make things that are revelant to us; we are not going to participate
in anything that you would offer that is less than that. They took that very
hard. We came into an era of Black picture making.

The first film that came out was a thing called COTTON COMES TO HARLEM and
we flocked to that and it went absolutely through the roof and all of a sudden
the banks of America began to rattle and the stock market on Wall Street began to
show different calculations because most of the motion picture industries are owned
by other industries. They're part of a conglomerate and these conglomerates began to
show all kinds of new profits out of their entertainment divisions.

Then, we had the VAN PEEBLE   film, SWEET SWEETBACK'S BAADASSSSS SONG and
that went through the roof, further than anything else. Then, they came right
back with SHAFT, then they came right back with SUPERFLY,and then something
began to happen to me. I began to see that once again, we were in a trap, and
what was that trap; the trap was that the Black community, wholly, passionately,
and decisively declared what it was prepared to do. Declared that it was prepared
to put its soul and its heart in what it was prepared to support and we began to
play games with that, instead of seizing upon this noble moment to begin to project
those things which would tell us about our history.

The hell with Tarzan and swinging through the trees and looking like
monkeys . Tell us about TIMBUCKTU,and the great university that existed when it
was the only important center of learning for a long, long time. And you kept
telling us of primitive people with savage conduct. Tell us about TIMBUCKTU; tell
us about the great ZULU warriors, who fought off the English and fought off the
Dutch and the great nobility that they put into that. Tell us a little about
that history! Tell us about HENRI CHRISTOPHE AND HAITI and TOUSSAINT L'OUVERTURE
and how, had it not been for them fighting the French army and defeating them to
a standstill, white folks would never been able to write about Waterloo and what
happened to NAPOLEON and how WELLINGTON won. 'Cause nowhere in their books, did
they ever tell you about..noway in hell could NAPOLEON have won that war in
WELLINGTON because his soldiers were dead, fighting slaves in HAITI. They don't
tell you that!

So, when I went on a campaign, I started to say-much to the annoyance of
many of my brothers-, I said,"That I cannot, no matter what you require of me,
stand up anywhere in life..and that you're gonna give me as my hero, a black
dope pusher and all you ask me to do (applause) is support him. Support him
because he happens to be in confrontation with a white cop, who is also filled
with injustices! Listen man, you ain't givin' me no choice. I don't like the
white cop whose a rip-off and I don't like the Black dope pusher...and I ain't
got no time to think about race. If you're asking about brotherhood, solidarity
and at the time giving me a whole lot of B.S. under the banner that we are all
Black together; we are only Black together when it's going down right and I
stopped being your (applause) kind of Blackness, when you start talking about
ripping off the Black Community and not giving a thought to what's important to
the growth of that community. So, we had a long dialogue on that and a guy
said to me,"Well, that's easy for you to say man, because you've made yours.
Yeah, it's alright sitting there in that posture having found some economic sec-
urity. I'm just tryin' to get a job, that's all I'm doing; I'm working!"
I said to him,"I'm gonna tell ya something, don't look at where I am; look
at where I come from too. I was a janitor on 143rd street and I was a janitor
at 555 Edgecombe (sugar hill). I was the janitors assistant,'cause my step-

father was the janitor (laugh) and I hauled the garbage and I fired the boilers and when I, fell in love with the AMERICAN NEGRO THEATRE on 126th street and 5th Avenue I decided that I wanted to be an artist.

I wanted work too, but when they told me that I had to go out and play an uncle tom; I decided I'd rather haul garbage. So don't gimme no stuff and tell me that you are working and that you have the right to work and that's all you are doing. At the price that you're paying, stay poverty stricken, if you have to sell your soul and sell your dignity in order to make a dollar. I don't see it! I can't buy it! I donot like alot of the T.V. series that I see on television, I just don't! I don't know what it means to the community...all I know is, that 20 years ago; we were fighting to keep the Beulahs of the world and the Mantan Morlans of the world, out of our lives. Some weird thing has taken place.

I now look out - I don't like The SANFORD AND SON SHOW. Sure it's funny sometimes but I don't like the debasement of it! Why is a Black woman, every time I look at SANFORD AND SON always the object of some vicious piece of humor? She's either a money grubbin', - you know - dirty old wrench, whose tryin' to break up some kind of a suggested homosexual relationship between the father and son. I don't buy it (applause) ! Don't tell me about THAT'S MY MAMA! My MAMA don't look like that! My MAMA don't talk like that! My MAMA'S, a much more dignified lady and her aspirations are infinitely more noble than the situations you're givin' me on T.V.! So, what kind of number is everybody runnin' on us now? The number is exploitation, profit and greed (clap) and we have to know how to become exempt from that when we're talking about ourselves; because we are not exempt from all kinds of human weaknesses.

SPIRITUALITY OF BLACK FOLKS. I believe that there's a magnificant spirituality to Black people. I believe that, not just from my experiences here but from the many, many, many hours, weeks, months and years that I have spent going from one end of AFRICA to another. I've had the joy of sitting down at the table of the Black president, a Black cabinet, a Black police force, a Black culture; Black women and Black men and children walking in the streets freely and never having to worry. What a noble experience that is! I wish I could put everybody in a boat for a week and lets go take a look at it. It's good for the soul. But I have to also keep in mind that LUMUMBA was one of the most important leaders that has ever come out of AFRICA was killed by Black men; as the tool of white oppression. I have to look at TOM MBOYA , what an absolutely incredible human being he was, coming out of KENYA working as hard as he did to get the grandfather of African Revolution GENERAL KENYATTAto get KENYA free. He brought alot of African students here, that we funded-that we made scholarships for- that he raised money for, that I spent time with. It's good to go back and see them after six, seven years, now sitting down and serving their country. I saw them when they first came here and now I see them sitting in government.

It was Black people that killed TOM MBOYA. What a maganificent man MALCOLM X was! What a gift he had! He turned me around so many times; I got up reeling. You know, sure it was the tools of the instrument of an oppressive society that did away with him. But it was Black Folks that killed. Now, what we've got to do is, we got to take a real good hard look at the measure of where we are. To really truly begin to evaluate what we want to extract from this society and what we are going to demand of our men and women who sit in the front, brothers who are the image makers. Those who sit down and are constantly used by white folks as the ears of what Black folks want. They never want to come to Black folks and hear because Black folks would tell them the truth too often.

22

It always goes against what is their interest so they go to these niggers. They sit there and try to talk on the country.

I was in that trap too. Yeah..I was. When I first started out, I was one of the most elegant cat you ever seen. I was so succinct, the words were so beautifully formulated. I could rap on any subject...but where the hell was I going? So I shifted gears and when I shifted gears they didn't want to hear from me too much after that. But they can't stop it, it's even bigger than them. Its got so sick they can't even keep their own houses in order. Look at NIXON and ROCKEFELLER and everybody. Right down the drain.... (applause). So, I find myself in this moment of life making new accessments, making new evaluations and in those new accessments and new evaluations I've said, I've had enough of that other platform. I want to go out and learn and to revitalize myself and to extract once again from the humblest sources those instances of truth and meaning that will help purify me as an artist and help shape how I am to use my life from here on in.

So, I have been to the RIKERS ISLAND; I went for 3 weeks on the Indian Reservation; I went to New Mexico and Arizona and I sat with my Indian brothers from Wounded Knee. I went to the federal courts where they're being tried and I sat and watched American justice at work. I sat with them, The Santo Domingo tribe; with the Navajo tribe; with the Zumi tribe; with the Kochati tribe and I watched what happened to them and I found one thing. That what's happening to the Indian in the U.S.A. is absolutely no different than what's happening to us and from the same people. They are our brothers; they are our sisters; we are as much in need of them, as they are of us and we've got to try to make that unity work. What is it that plagues the Indian more than anything else? You have no idea how bad alcoholism is...dope is there too, but alcohol is a little cheaper. So there they sit being ripped off by alcohol and here we sit being ripped off by heroin! And who's doing it? The same cat! How do we stop being divided among ourselves, those who are the victims of oppression? How do we make a coalition here that brings forth a new truth and a new day?...and we have the power to do that!

I was absolutely overjoyed when Narco took the position he did on that movie. What was the name of that movie? COME BACK CHARLESTON BLUE. If it comes out and it ain't right, PICKET IT! Because the one thing they will not do and don't let nobody put this trip on you; they ain't gonna stop makin' Black pictures. Not as long as Black people have some money to spend. They'll let you see what you want. But you've got to let them know what you want because if you accept everything they give you, they ain't gonna give you what's good for your soul or good for your head. They will continue to give you that which will keep you in the dark without dignity, without a sense of self. All we have to do is hear from you. Believe me, it has vast power. The minute those people in hollywood know that nigga's ain't buyin' no more SUPER FLY'S; they ain't buyin' no more super women doing all kinds of karate chops and leapin' off (laugh) building. I've never seen that in all my life. On the screen I saw a whole new thing, it was almost as good as Tarzan swinging through the trees. I want to see something that tells me what we really are, and that we owe ourselves and that we can do it. It ain't no rip-off either. It can make it, as long as Black people-they'll make anything you want to see. The only time they'll stop making it is when you all stop spending money to go see anything. Then they ain't gonna bother. That's the power you have.

Fragments of a Spritual

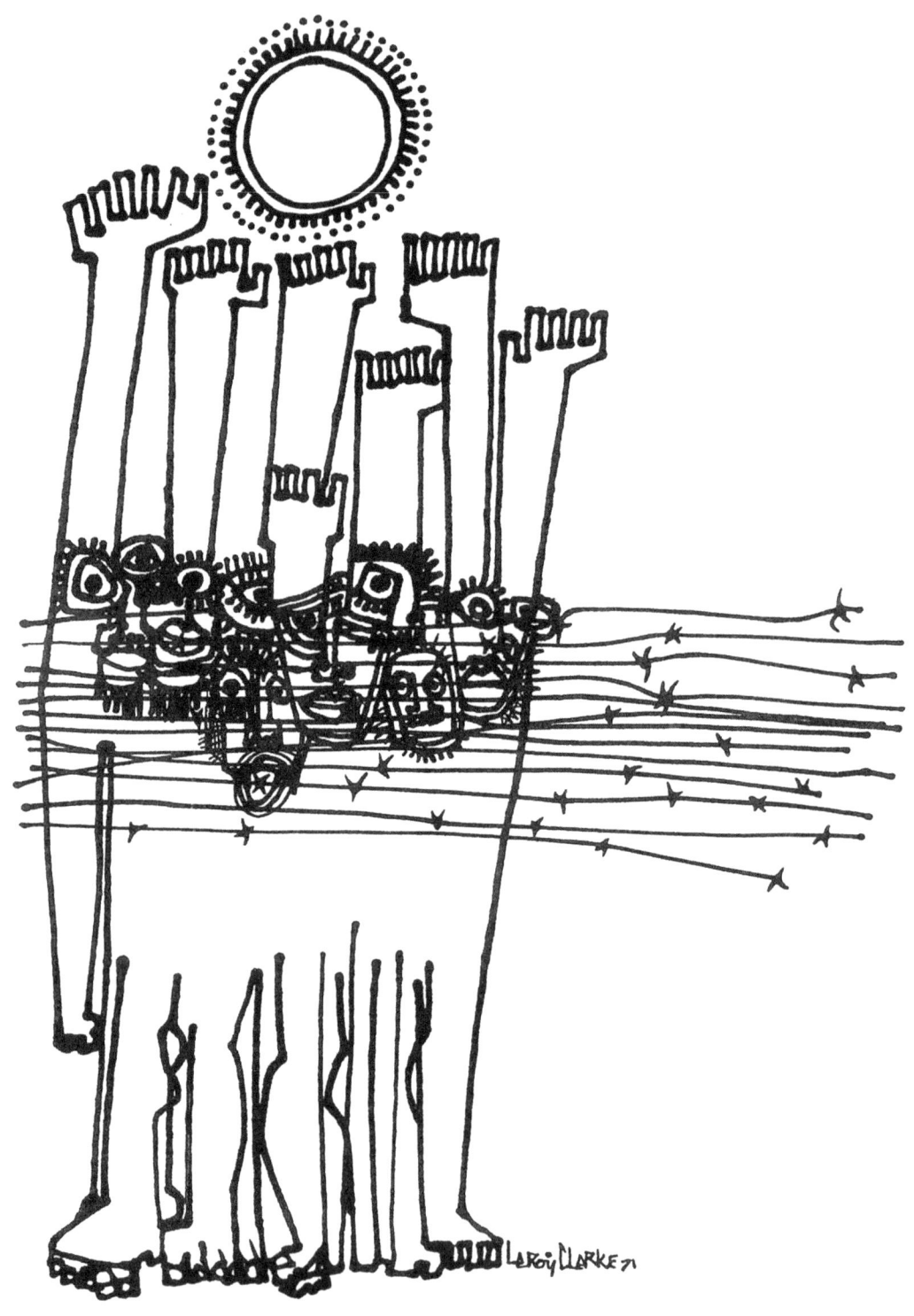

LeRoy Clarke 71

GOAT BITE

(for Louise and Cecelia)

Yuh little beast,
Playing yuh can't give meh peace.
Boy ah tired wid yuh,
Come here,
Yuh little good for nothing
Just like yuh father
Just like yuh runaway father
That dirty so and so, scamp.
Look, I can't take it no more nuh
He give me yuh, and gorn.
Now like you come to finish the job
Yuh want to kill meh before meh time
And send meh to meh grave.
Well yuh lie,
I go kill you first, wid blows
Yuh doh want to do nothing in the place
Just eat sleep and shit.
Come here yuh lil' vagabond
Come here ah tell yuh
Work night and day to mind you
And bring yuh up
Now what ah get,
Eh, what ah get?

For all the hard times ah had to endure
Sun and rain, braking dew, cold, hot.
Night come, day go
Some days ah have nothing to eat
Some nights ah have less
What more ah could do for you?
Ah going almost naked to put shoe on yuh foot.
Yuh dirty father never give meh a cent
I had to pay for everything and rent.
On top it all yuh 'car' give meh peace
Ah send yuh to school to give yuh some education
For yuh to come out something good
Yuh run 'way from school, break biche
Go in the patch to catch dove
Go in the hills for mango
Yuh like yuh want nothing good
Look at yuh cousin John
He pass exhibition, now he going to Q.R.C. college.
College yes!
He go come out some doctor, or big time lawyer.
He mother could be proud ah he!
Like goat bite me,
Eh boy, tell meh, goat bite me eh, eh?
Answer meh, goat bite meh?
- Yess...Nno...mammy.

LeRoy Clarke

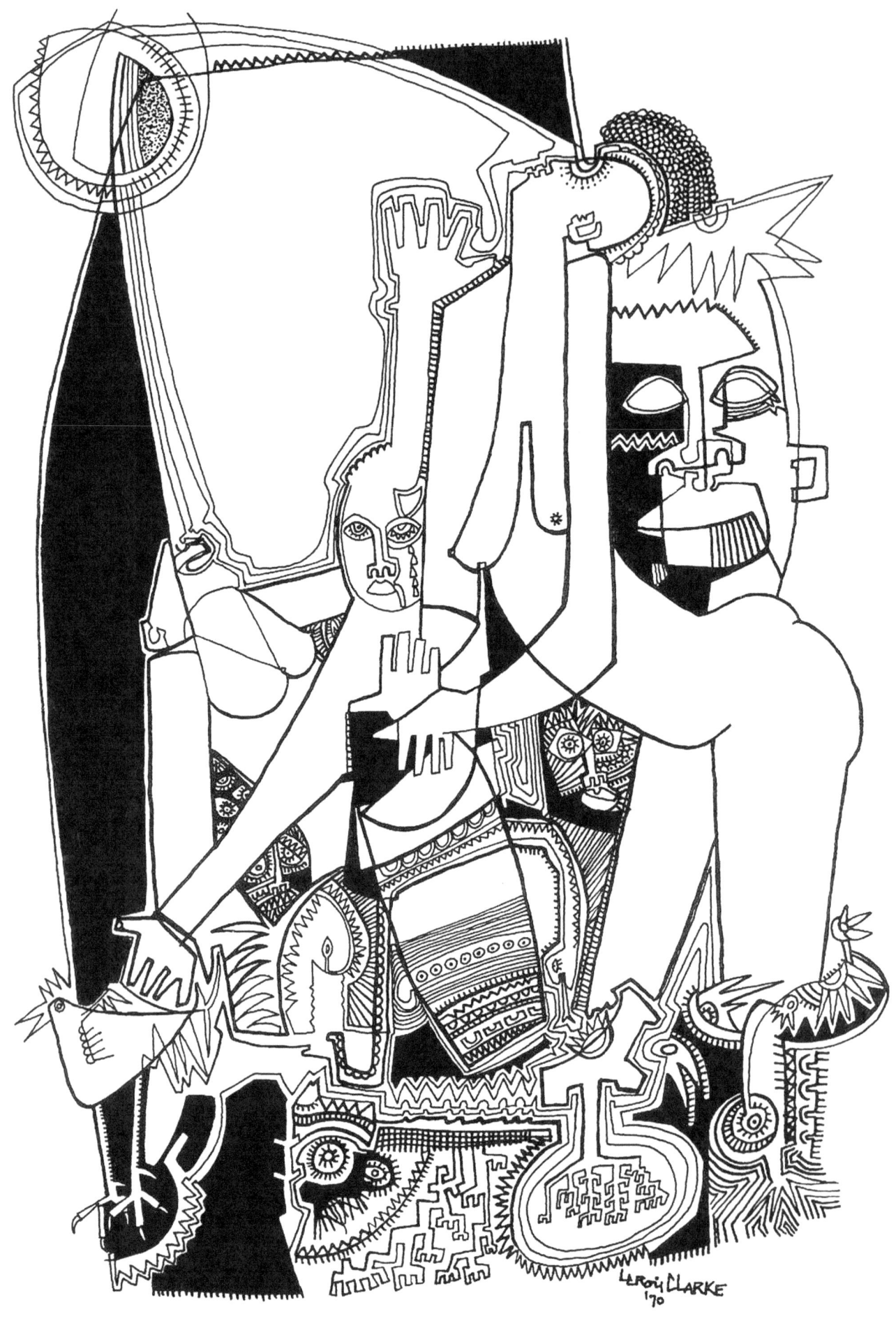

SONG FOR A WASTED WOMAN

I

CONVICTION

Call me old woman and barren,
wet fire-wood.
A heap of broken clayware
with puddles of tears
too muddy to breed tadpoles.
But I say to you;
when my youth danced its skirts
across the fields,
my toes picked notes on stones
too smoothe for moss to grow,
I laughed at love, yes,
once like you I was honey-dew,
full and overflowing, just like you.
Luring men with burning throats
to quench to heart-desire at my lips;
made their senses drunk, that
they rent the bush to my delight.
How quickly I spat their warm sweetness,
I long for a poking through the rust.
Old woman, and barren: they say.

II

A PRAYER..(for child-bearing..)

Two-score and five years have so
etched my brow with furrows of dispair,
my greying head begins
to droop in the fun of my eyes.
The mask of unanswered prayers
scars my faith.
Body of mine cradling the pain of
the dry rattle-song,
isn't the womb cursed
that knows not a single growth?

Great gods who fashion the way
for countless brides deserving:
Tell me where the sin occurred
that your scorn wrapped in
bitter-sweet maids resolves
to mock my womanhood.
I beseech this chance
that I might undo this curse.

Say, in sacrifice
I lay here before you.
Rape me like the careless spark
that fires a vestal forest.
Raise my skirts with your burning tongues
that animals trampling out
will unrest this sleep.

Rain on the ashes of my charred blood
fresh seed to root its manure.
Great gods,
I postulate a harbour of dry shells.
Come, fill me!

III

A DREAM..(she is pregnant..)

....nine moons have now crossed the sky,
where alas, no blood dates the trail.
I a ploughed field, marked
with careful plodding
walk to greet with perfumed blooms
kisses of the pollen beak;
life's nectar swells my breasts
which like sand-bags before,
lay waste on some shore...

...Here I rest,
dance in me child of my evening,
skip your feet that will split the bonds
that enslaved my years.
Chase butterflies that bopped in my emptiness,
till flattened between your clumsy fingers
I am brushed off the idle women's gossip
in a little boy's ear.

Carry my voice dilly-dallying in your play
to mix with other mothers', crying
their children home in the late evening.
Reach up my neck and kiss my cheeks
where a glistening silver thread
marks the tear I wept for your safe keep.
Come, rest with me.......

LeRoy Clarke

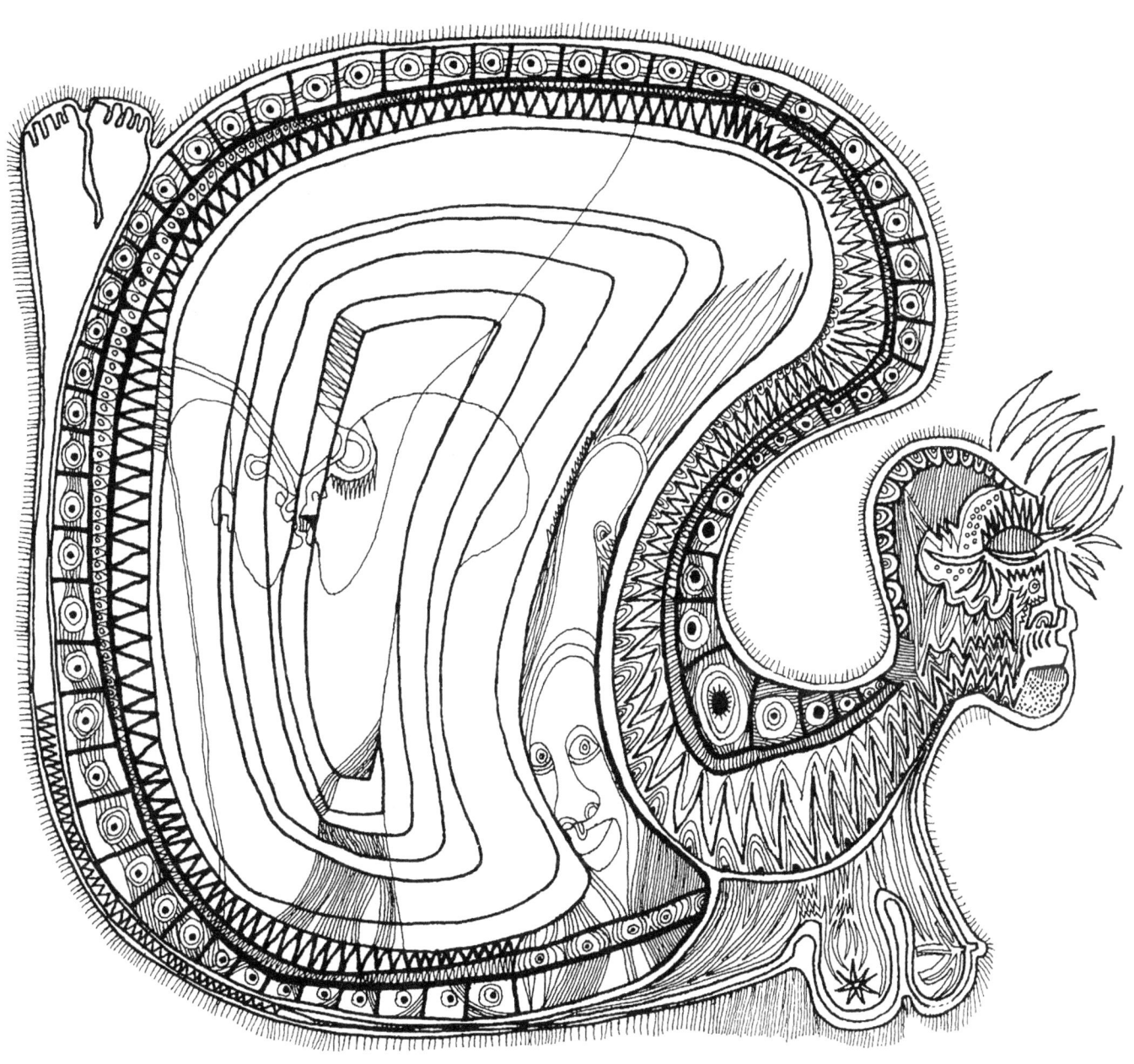

"MEAT ON THE BONE"

by David Jackson

The beauty of Taj Mahal and his music is that both totally reflect the full spectrum of Black life. "I don't define myself," says Taj when talking about all the kinds of music he does. "I'm just a man on the planet Earth with very definite roots that go to Africa and that's all I know. The rest of it is just somebody's else's mischief."

Elaborating further he says, "I like the way you can look at what's a part of your heritage and all the different things that make individual types of people. Music is the most expressive form of the different people, and you can absorb all these people by learning to play their forms of music, which is the absolute expression of who they are."

Taj Mahal is a serious student of Black life, an Afro-American folk musician, "an authentic carrier," to quote Kalamu Ya Salaam, "of our culture, the total way in which we live (culture) that's happening everyday."

A self-styled ethomusicologist, Taj is apt to perform a piece, say like, Blind Willie McTell's "Statesboro Blues", an eastern Georgia product of African and British Traditions, then follow that with "Cajun Waltz" which reveals the interplay of African and French traditions in Louisiana. In Taj's music and lifestyle are references to blues, field calls and cries, field songs, fishing songs, railroad songs, preaching-singing styles, ring shots, jazz, rhythm & blues, reggae, and other West Indian songs. A musician of far-ranging skills; Taj often accompanied himself on slide guitar, electric guitar, banjo, mandolin, harp, aucostic bass piano, kalimba, conch shell, and other percussive devices. He is also a master of the arts of whistling and hamboning.

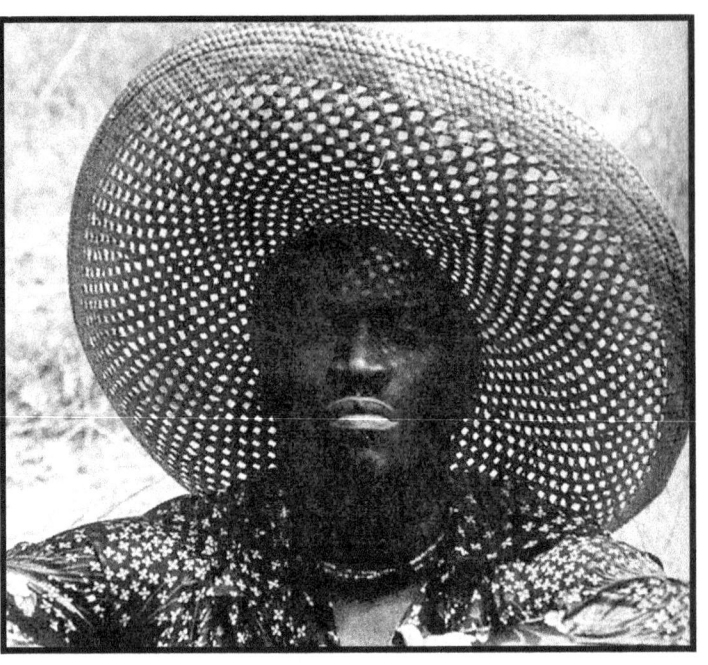

Taj Mahal
Photo courtesy Columbia Records

This wide field of vision was reflected recently when Taj appeared at Manhattan's Bottom Line Club. With his beautiful personality, his stimulating presence, his arsensal of instruments, and knowledge of his roots as extensive as any "bog-dwelling" Mississippi hoodoo doctor; Taj, like a "spirit in the dark," entered the heads of the people on hand for his performances and possessed their souls. A cake walking, funky butt-shakin', guiding spirit, he took the people outside their minds to that land of strange and beautiful "fits" where that big-legged, sweet brown skin mama, Corinna, with her fabled jellyroll, and that old "heathen" good, good lovin' "good thang" strut their stuff.

Taj started each set playing an adaption of Mississippi John Hurt's soothing "I'm Satisfied", an eloquent song which says: "I'm satisfied and tickled, too, baby to know I'm in love with you."

After doing the hamstring poppin' "Cake walk Into Town" and two other solo numbers, accompanying himself on electric quitar, Taj brought out his new band. The musicians include: Hoshal Wright, guitarist; Luther Cuffy, bassist; Kester Smith, trap drums; Larry McDonald, percussionist; Rudy Costa, woodwinds, flute and kalimba.

"This next song," Taj says, "is dedicated to all freshman women and others in pursuit of higher education." He and the band jumped into the classic "Good Morning Lil' School Girl," bringing to mind some old lecherous blood on 116th street crackin' on some young sister on her way to school: "Good morning lil' school girl, can I go home with you?"

Next they performed "Going Up to The Country, Paint My Mailbox Blue," with Taj playing some basic homegrown harmonica in the tradition of Sonny Roy Williamson and Little Walter. Although the band recycled some of the older stuff-including, in addition to the tunes already mentioned, the Memphis Jug Band's "Stealin', Stealin'" which was dedicated to the up and coming depression, "Shady Grove," and "Fishin' Blues"-they mostly played songs from Taj's new Columbia album, "MO' ROOTS": "Why Did You Have To Desert Me?", "Blackjack Davey," "Cajun Waltz," and "Johnny Too Bad."

"MO ROOTS" stems from Taj's personal experiences with Jamaican music and is essentially dedicated to his father, who was of West Indian parentage.

Not all the songs on the album are original tunes by Taj. "Slave Driver " was written by Jamaican writer-performer Robert Marley of the popular group, Bob Marley and the Wailers. "Desperate Lover" and "Johnny Too Bad" are reggae tunes originating in Jamaica. Marley also collaborated on the mixing of the album with Taj, who also produced it.

"Why Did You Have to Desert Me?", "Clara (St. Kitts Woman)" and "Big Mama," are all original tunes by Taj Mahal. "Blackjack Davey" and "Cajun Waltz" are adaptions. In speaking of "Waltz" which some so-called purists might say is a Louisiana Cajun tune and shouldn't be included on a composite West Indian music album, let me just point out that the music of French speaking Louisiana Black people relates more closely to the culture of the French West Indies than to that of the U.S. in general. Not only does the tune fit in with the rest, but it is, in my opinion, one of the best on the album, second only to "Why Did You Have To Desert Me?".

Black people have just recently started to respond to Taj's music, for whatever reasons. One of the reasons why Blacks didn't initially get into Taj's music (he has been on the scene a long time) is because, in his own words, "...my music sounds like the music of an illiterate man." In an interview with Mark Rosenberg in University Review, Taj goes on to say, "White people understand the value of it, but they don't move. The classical background of Western people is to hear a symphony and sit there and applaud. When you listen to Black Music it's involving you, surrounding you, demanding of you and on all levels of your being-and it's spiritual! It's for relieving the spirit and the mental health of the people. "Without it, people have problems." Black people are getting more and more into what Taj is doing, and into other Black musicians who aren't in the mainstream.

"MO ROOTS" is a good starting point for those who aren't hip to Taj Mahal."RECYCLING THE BLUES AND OTHER STUFF," "THE REAL THING (LIVE AT FILLMORE EAST)", and "OOOH SO GOOD 'N BLUES" are also recommended. They are available on Columbia Records. you're bound to love them some.

BLACK ART
AND
WHITE CRITICS

BY CALVIN WILSON

No matter how much the Black artist strives for artistic excellence in his work, he is always confronted with the problem of surviving in a materialistic society without compromising his own values. In order to speak to a Black audience truthfully, the Black artist must recognize the irrelevance of commercial values; unfortunately, while economic considerations are restrictive to artistic expression, they can never be ignored.

As the Black artist works to influence the minds of his people, he is constantly at odds with the largest and most influential communications network in the world. More Black people watch television and read the popular national magazines than will ever attend a performance of NO PLACE TO BE SOMEBODY or read an issue of THE BLACK SCHOLAR. While it may be said that the American public as a whole is not inclined towards the arts and/or academic journals, the fact remains that the position of Black people is more urgent than that of the average american. In order for Black Art to survive, it must have the support of the people. Thus, the incredible power of the mass media becomes a very real and dangerous threat. As an example of this, think of the many Black people who have read THE EXORCIST but have not read THE AUTOBIOGRAPHY OF MALCOLM X.

Black theatre particularly has been a victim of the mass media's concept of art. This mass media concept calls for big, luxurious theaters, high-priced tickets and what is commonly referred to as "painless entertainment." Almost all Broadway and many Off Broadway shows are geared to the rich and upper middle class, and as a result much of the general public thinks of theater as nothing more than a pleasant diversion. Black people particularly have been victims of the mass media's judgemental arm, white critics. Since the playwright can speak to the people only through the contents of his plays, he has no way of getting them to come see the play in order to be exposed to his ideas. The playwright must rely upon word-of-mouth and the critics. Since there is not yet a large Black theater audience, word-of-mouth is scarce. And since in the major newspapers and magazines that Black people read the theater reviews are written by white critics, the reviews are biased against the concept of the Black aesthetic. Since these critics are all coming out of a Broadway bag, however, it's hard to see how their reviews could possibly relate to any concept of Black Art, anyway.

It is not impossible, however, for a white critic to like a Black play for the wrong reasons. And when the play is good or excellent, as THE RIVER NIGER was, it can be a good thing. THE RIVER NIGER well deserved the praise it got from any critics, Black or white. The most important factor in terms of the Black artist and community was the art of the play, while the white critics and theatergoers thought of it more in terms of the traditional "well-made play," some critics even comparing it to the works of Chekhov. But in this case the most significant virtue was that the playwright, Joseph A. Walker, saw his play attended by many Black people. Black Art, though on Broadway, was still Black Art.

Recently another Black playwright, Richard Wesley, did not fare as well. Wesley's newest play, THE SIRENS, was presented at the Manhattan Theater Club under the co-production of Wesley himself and equally accomplished Black playwright Ed Bullins. THE SIRENS dealt with the relationship of the Black woman to the Black man through the story of a Newark prostitute whose husband has deserted her ten years before the action of the play begins. Not only do we get a full picture of the drives which move this sister to act as she does, but also a detailed outline of the notions of sex roles which dictate the course of sexual conduct in our community. All of the characters were fully realized and totally believable. Beyond the extreme credibility of the characters, the actors which interpreted them were all superb, most notably Loretta Greene. In the role of the main character's younger sidekick (also a prostitute), sister Greene endowed her character with a sense of being so striking that one could almost believe she would actually be the character upon walking off the stage. The entire production was well designed, with jazz interludes in the background which provided a perfect accompaniment to the mood of the play. It was a play of tremendous value not only as entertainment but also, and more importantly, as an analysis of Black life. Unfortunately, its location at an Off-Off Broadway theater on the east side, remote from the Black community, might have been a deterrent to Black audiences. Probably far more crippling to the play's attendance was the reaction of white critics who either spoke of the "stereotypes" Wesley employed or made statements which sounded like this: "The play may be about the Black experience but it's really about the human experience." The inability of these critics to comprehend the racism of such a statement stands as a monument both to their stupidity and ignorance.

It's no news that no matter how fine his work is, the Black playwight is always referred to as "promising" or worse by the white critics, even if he's been writing for many years and has many fine accomplishments to his credit. This is not to say that the Black playwright either seeks or needs white approval. As Melvin Van Peebles so perceptively put it, there's no point in the Black playwright's lookin' for justice because there isn't any justice.

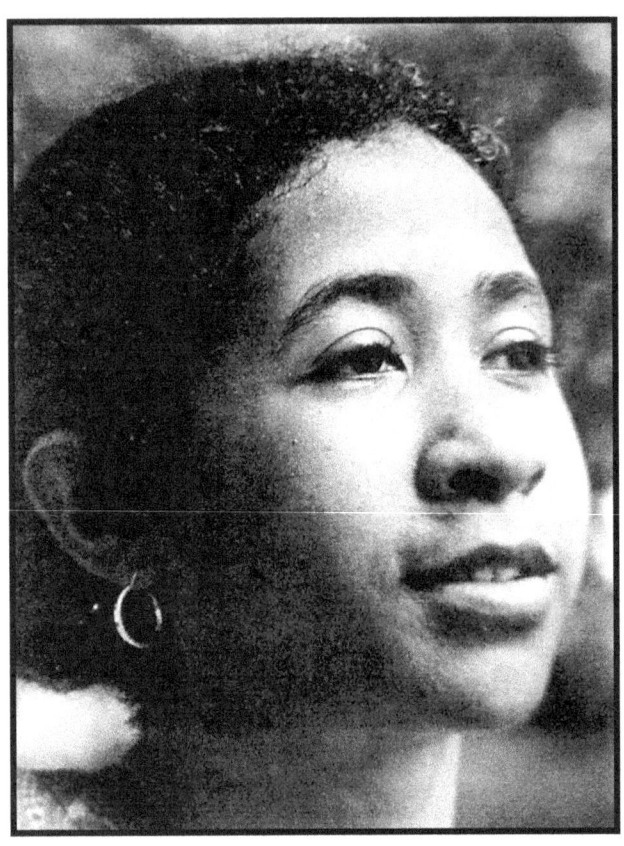

MOVIN'

BY PAT GLENN

Interview with Dianne McIntyre, Choreographer of

SOUNDS IN MOTION

Dance Company

Pat: I'm really interested in your early childhood, the kinds of things you did as a child, the schools you went to and more importantly how you got started in dance.

Diane: Well, I'm from Cleveland, Ohio originally and I was dancing as long as I can remember long before I started any kind of formal training. My mother says that I used to dance around the house and you know I can remember that! I've always danced. But I had alot of other things I was interested in also at the time I didn't know as a child that I wanted to be a dancer. I knew that I wanted to dance but I didn't know I wanted to do that professionally. But, you know I wanted to be a nurse at one time, an interior decorator, a translator, an architect ...you name it.

Pat: How about now, do you have any other outside interests other than dance?

Diane: Well, I think that most of the things that I'm interested in besides dance feed into my dances because I'm interested in the world and people and us as a people, especially our roots and heritage- "where we came from," and I've been doing as much reading as I can on those kind of subjects. So all of that comes out in my dances.

Pat: Have you done any acting?

Diane: No, not formally.

Pat: There's one dance that you do; I can't recall the name of it, but it's a solo and the character looks just like a junkie.

Diane: Bessie Smith.

Pat: Right...and you fall right into it so nicely like you've taken acting lessons.

Diane: Well that's a part of what a dancer has to be, an actress at the same time. Sometimes we must express ourselves just in terms of the line and movement in an abstract way. At other times we express ourselves as characters, so we have to be characters or part of the story. But I've never been into acting where I've had to talk. Yet I know that if I was into that kind of situation; I would do it as well as I could.

Pat: I'm sure you would. When did you start your company?

Diane: Well we first had our first performance in March '72 and I had auditioned at Clark Center. Louise Roberts - who is the director of Clark Center- suggested that if I was looking for people to work with, that I post signs concerning auditions, and I did but didn't expect there to be any response because people didn't know me - I had just come here. But people came, you know they came because people are interested in dancing and some of the people who are with me now- I found in the audition. Bernadine Jennings, was at that audition. Although I had known her just slightly before and Bill Donald I knew from Cleveland. Bill and I worked together before and Dorian Williams was kind of at the audition. She was on the telephone and I had seen her dance before and she told me that she was interested in working with us. Now there were about 8 dancers who came out of that audition, but those are the only 3 people who are still with me now.

Pat: How many are in your company now?

Diane: Right now we have 3 women and 4 permanent men. Two are new, they just auditioned a couple of weeks ago and we have one male in the company who is right now a guest artist; and I don't know how it will contend with him because he works for a couple of other companies. So at this time he's really tied up. But he's a good person and we'd like to do as much with him as we can.

Pat: Can you name the people in the company?

Diane: Right...there's Bernadine Jennings, Lonnetta Gaines, Linda Griffin, William Donald, Victor Braxton. Charles Grant is the guest artist with us who also works for Eleo Pomare and our new people are Larry Dandlers and Horace Whitson and they have not performed with us yet but they will this weekend.

Pat: How did you decide on the name SOUNDS IN MOTION; it has such a nice rhythm to it ?

Diane: Thank you. Well the name first came out of me working with musicians. I was interested in working with musicians as another player. It was like my body was an instrument and we all played and related to each other in the way that musicians relate to each other. So that I felt that it's not only that way with music but it's my belief that that's what dance is. It's like the music moving and it's that kind of thing that I wanted to express, so that's where the name came from.

Pat: You have a drummer, Babafumi. Where did you meet him?

Diane: Alright, I was telling you the names of the company people, the musicians are part of the company also. So Babafumi Akunyun is also a company member. Steve Solder who's the trap drummer; Ahmed Abdullah, trumpet player; Gwendolyn Nelson is our singer and actress, she's the all around theater person. There are also permanent members of the company, two other people who were with us for awhile but who may come back. I can't say really what their state is right now: Dorian Williams is now dancing in Boston, Phillip Bond who is in the new production of the WIZ, yeah they're all from here! When he comes back he might be able to still work with us. We'll see how far we can move them up.

Pat: What style of dance do you do?

Diane: It's called Modern, but it's really not the name. I don't feel it's the correct title because Modern Dance is something that started in the 1920's, which sprung out of a revolution against a Classical Ballet style. What Modern Dance has become since then is so far away from that original thing and also each Modern Dancer is so stylistically different from the next Modern Dancer, that it's not like you can say Jazz Dancers or Ballet Dancer or Tap Dancer. There is an underlying thing that's the same with all of them, in his or her area. Modern Dancers are as different one to another as Ballet is from Tap Dance. It's difficult that we are all categorized as the same thing but there's not a better name - we've been called CONTEMPORARY DANCE also!

Pat: What do you prefer to call it?

Diane: I just call it Modern, but I prefer not to call it anything.

Pat: ...not to put it into any category?

Diane: Right, but that's what it's called.

Pat: Do you combine dance styles, like Modern with Ballet or Jazz?

Diane: It could look like that, but

see we've been influenced by all those different areas but it's not specifically what we try to do. 'Cause you know, I've had classes in those other areas- but it's not what I work for. I'm not working for a combination of these things. It just what comes out.

Pat: Where have you performed in the past and where do you have planned performances in the future?

Diane: Well, since our company is new, we've performed mostly here in the New York City area. Our first performance was in the Cubiculo theater; a small theater on 61st street. We did a couple of performances at Clark Center; two years we were there. We've been performing 2 years in all and we have performed in public schools at all levels and at community centers. This summer we did many outdoor performances; we were at Lincoln Center and at the Delacorte Theater and out in Queens and on the Dance Mobile and at the New Harlem Cultural Center. Last week we were at the University of Massachusetts and we're doing a demonstration at Yale week after next. So we're beginning to so some college things. We were at Barnard 2 weeks ago, and this year again we'll be at the Harlem Cultural Center hopefully and at Hunter. I think our biggest production of the year in the city will be at Hunter and also at Henry Street.

Pat: Going off on a different tangent, what about performing out of the country, have you given much thought about dancing in Africa or Europe for example?

Diane: At this point, we're just taking things one step at a time. I'm interested first in us building up a real strong base here and that has to do with booking and our administration has to be very strong. Besides I want to go other places in this country first. There are alot of people here who haven't seen too much dance at all. I'm doing a residency thing at Alabama with Affiliate Artists right now and some of the people there are trying to get into my company in the spring. So that we're first trying to do a southern tour, then after that we go to the mid-west.

Pat: Can you tell me about that residency in Alabama?

Diane: Sure. I'm with an organization called AFFILIATE ARTISTS. The Affiliate Artists is a New York based organization. They have auditions for artists and then they have institutions around the country, either art institutions or schools or community centers or church organizations that are interested in bringing artists to the community. The artists based at this place do what is called informances or what is called informal performances at places all around that area of the institution. Also the artist teaches classes and gives workshops to people in the area. So, it's like bringing the artist and the people together. That's what the theme of the Affiliate Artists really is and it's to bring the art into areas that it might not go otherwise.

Pat: So you're commuting back and forth?

Diane: Right. I'll go there 4 times over the year altogether. I went my first time in the middle of October and I'll go again in November and then again in Febuary and in April. I'll go for about 2 weeks at a time, so it's like an 8 week program.

Pat: O.K., I'd like to get into your choreography now. This is a question that I've been trying to shape clearly. When you're creating a piece, what do you go through? Does it just come out; do you dream about it; do you have a concept in your head then you try to express it?

Diane: Well, they come in different ways. When I was in school and when I was choreographing just for myself and it wasn't for a deadline for some performance, things would come and what I'd call movement would come to me or I'd hear a piece of music that I thought was nice or there was something that I wanted to dance about, so I would just start working on that. Now since I've had my company, there are some things that I've been interested in doing, not only because they are things that spring out of me but something that had to do with the dancers or the individuals involved with the company. Because we have musicians, I'm interested in doing things which will bring the musicians out as well as the dancers and have them to do it with their particular instrument. That would naturally affect what the dance will be like, but still have both things where things spring up in me. I'm interested in like what I was saying before, in our heritage, so that anything that will come out of it about Black people, in terms of our music or in terms of what we we're about, not necessarily in the Arts world but in the past; those are the things that really interest me. You know, sometimes I really feel that I've lived at another time and not only that, but that I understand how it was and that I was really there. So that's why a lot of the emphasis on what I do comes from the past. It can be an educational thing for people who see us, not only Black people but also other non-Black people, educating them to what we were about in the past. Sometimes I have ideas about things that I want to say that has to do with today and today's world and I think it is possible to apply structure in a dance without it being a tool for it. If it can come out and flow and not look like something that's trying to preach to people. But then I do pieces also that come out of a mood or that doesn't necessarily have a implied message or statement; so that it has to do with movement that I think is important or nice or some kind of movement that I think other choreographers possibly have been missing and something that I think is important-that's a vital part of who we are too, just as the way we move is part of us.

Pat: I know that you choreographed The Great McDaddy, that must have been a trip in itself. Did you have a script to go by; did you have it prearranged as to what they wanted you to do?

Diane: Well, that was really an interesting thing because another person who usually works with the Negro Ensemble Company was supposed to do this choreography but at the last minute they found out that he couldn't do it. We had done a performance the last year before and one of their staff people had seen our company and they noticed that I did scenes from the 1920's and The Great McDaddy was set mostly in the 20's, so that's why they suggested me. We talked with Douglas Turner Ward- the director of not only the production but of the theater- he felt that I was somebody who might be able to do it. He showed me the script by Paul Carter Harrison and I read it and Doug told me the things that he was interested in seeing and that he didn't want the pieces in this particular play to be like production numbers. He wanted all of it to flow together. That was really interesting for me because I didn't have to go against the things that I believe in. Production numbers in musicals sometimes break the whole intent of what the thing is supposed to be about. So this was right up my line. After he told me what he wanted, was interested in, I was free to do what I wanted. Then, when he saw it, if it wasn't fulfilling of what he thought the whole piece should be about, I then would make changes and he would tell me about it.

Pat: Would you be interested in choreographing for plays again?

Diane: You mean another piece? Yes, I would be. If it had the same kind of integrity, where I thought it was a play that was saying some positive things. There are some things that, unfortunately, aren't as deep as they could be. Some of it is too superficial. It would be hard for me to get involved in that kind of production, even if there was a lot of money. Of course, I could do turns and kicks and whatever stuff, but it's not what I'd want my stamp put on.

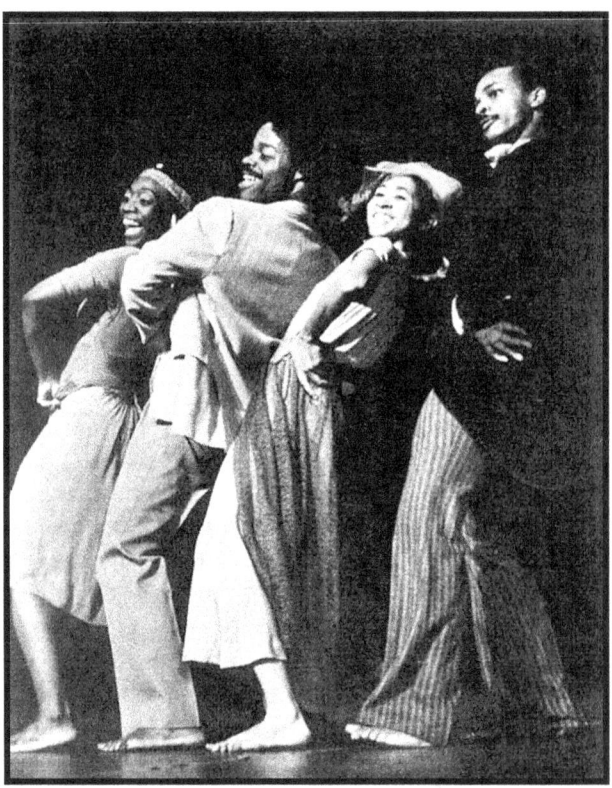

Pat: Right! What kind of feedback do you get from the audience when you're performing?

Diane: The audience is always very positive and enthusiastic. I can't remember a time when it hasn't been. Now, depending who the audience is, they're more enthusiastic than other types of people. We did a thing at

NET once and the performances were very powerful. This piece called "Smoking Cloud", the dancers really did it! But the people in the audience wasn't ready for it; it was very close in range to them. You know, It really frightened them; the response was very subdued. But, I don't know, it made me happy because I knew that it must of hit them. But then not to respond... It hit them and they understood what we were sayin', 'cause in the end, the dancer ends up very angry. Different responses depend upon the age group of the people. There's also feed-back from people who come back-stage and talk to us. That's very helpful for me when people say what they got out of something. How it's affecting them? That's really-besides the dancers and the musicians, who I love, all of them-but besides their enthusiasim, those things that people come back and tell me are one of the things that keeps me going and going on to the next level. 'Cause I know that we've touched people in some way and that this headache is worth it...

Pat: Getting into critics, you know there's a great deal of talk about how white critics donot understand Black dancers or Black plays; how do you feel about that?

Diane: Now in most of my experience, I've had experience being in the dance world and having write ups. Yet it's really a new thing for me. To have a performance where we think it just knocks people out and it did-that you were knockin' the audience out, and for the reviewer not to say that...Not that the reviewer is negative but that sometimes he just doesn't capture with the words, what the event was really like. The review may be cold, really cold and we had something like that happen recently. We were at the Delacorte Theater and we performed on the program with four companies. All the companies performed very well and there was a Spanish company on the program too. But the Spanish company and our company, like I think the audience response was closer and just bigger. Yet the reviews said the least and the most negative things about the two of us. It was not the way it had happened! But then I understand that Clive Barnes, who writes often for Dance and theater-he's never seen us-doesn't go to a play unless he knows something about the background of the playwright and he sees the play several times before he writes about it. He sees it in rehearsal or during previews and when he feels capable of writing about it he then talks to to the author or the choreographer, whatever. It's something that they have to get into. You just can't go one time cold and then feel that you can write about it. Critics must realize that they are dealing with livelihoods and careers which they affect by the things that they write. It's very important to understand what's happening, especially if it's something that some people who have not grown up out of the experience that they have. So then they have to try to understand what that experience is and to understand how it's different from theirs. So that, if they feel they're confident enough to write about it, then they have to know what they're talking about.

Pat: Do you deal with alot of improvisation in your dances?

Diane: All right, some part of my dances. Not as much as people might think because I try to make things look spontaneous. That's choreography! Improvisation is very important in dance and it doesn't happen enough. Dancers should be allowed to improvise even within a structure more freely because they have a whole creative thing inside of them. Of course, a dancer is always creative, taking the movement you give them

39

and making it their own. But besides that, they can come up with movement spontaneously on the spot and it could be very exciting. It can also be awful dangerous 'cause it can be terrible, you know, it could just not happen. But when it does happen it is very exciting. That's the kind of thing that we do with the musicians and dancers. When the music is alive and the dancers are the same.......

Pat: What do you recommend for an aspiring dancer, a new dancer?

Diane: Well, it depends on, well first the person should try to learn himself and learn about what he really wants to do. Anybody who thinks that they really want to dance, I suggest to them they just go out and try to do that. Dance is not necessarily a safe, secure area. But if they have a desire to go into dance and that they have a dancer inside of them-cause I've meet so many older people that have told me, "you know I was really interested in dance." It's a thing that if you don't get out there and try, you'll never know. It's kinda a rough life. I mean in this particular area of dance. You may not really want to do it, but if you don't get out there and try it; all your life you'll be wondering, wondering, if you should have ventured out into that area and done it. There'll always be a part of you that'll be unsettled and not satisfied, even if the rest of your life is very happy. They should just jump in and try.

Pat: Are you on a special diet or something?

Diane: Well, I don't think it's special. I don't eat meat and that was something that happened over time. I didn't jump up and say that I wanted to be a vegetarian. In fact, right now I don't call myself a vegetarian. I don't eat meat, but I think being a vegetarian is a category. It happened gradually. I started cutting out certain things. I'd stop fixing myself certain things for myself, then I would eat them when I was someplace and then I eventually I would not eat them when I went someplace. So it was like that gradual. I'm very interested in nutrition and how it affects the body. I've done quite a lot of reading in that area and talked to alot of people. Right now I get a lot of protein from nuts and I eat cereals, fruit and vegetables. Those kinds of things I eat. Sometimes I eat eggs and milk. It depends on how I feel. Sometimes when I feel I need it, I eat fish too. Mostly I eat fish out or if somebody has it. There was a time when I ate a lot of fish. Fish and rice. I eat alot of rice still, even though I have less and less time to use for fixing it

Pat: Would you fast before a performance?

Diane: Not before a performance. I've never tried that before a performance. If I did it would have to be awhile before a performance because during a fast you only start getting strong after a couple of days because you're kind of weak at the beginning. So I think that it would be very possible because sometimes the performing energy comes out of something else. It doesn't come out of what you eat.

Pat: What kinds of dance classes do you offer with SOUNDS IN MOTION?

Diane: Modern classes that I teach on Mondays and Wednesdays at 6 o'clock. Bernadine Jennings teaches a beginning modern class in Horton Techniques. There are not many people around who know Horton Technique.

Pat: What's Horton Techique?

Diane: Well, Horton is a technique that Alvin Ailey dance is based on	It was devised by I think Electra Horton, who is a native Californian. You know there's some dancers around today, who study with him and are influenced by him. So Bernadine teaches Horton. She studied with him and she teaches that on Thursday at 6 o'clock P.M. and Saturday at 1 o'clock. On Tuesday, at 6 o'clock we have a West African class by Papus Kamara and on Saturday at 10:30 .M. we have a ballet class taught by Harold Pierson. That's a very good class, that Ballet class on Saturday.

Pat: Where is the school located?

Diane: It's at 110 East 125th Street.

Pat: Just one last question...

Diane: Sure.

Pat: What is your experiences with the myth that dancing is just a feminine thing?

Diane: Well, in our company we're trying to wipe out that image. The men in dance really are the leaders today. You know, they're the directors and the choreographers, but only a few Black women choreograph right now. At first there were Carol Prince and Katherine Dunham were the Black choreographers, but the leaders in dance are really men. When I'm at Talla Dega in Alabama, that's the thing I try to emphasize to people who haven't seen much dance. That it's not a feminine thing and that young men should if they're interested get into dance as well as young women. But it was interesting because I didn't really have to emphasize that there. They were already interested in dancing, you know the young fellas were and it was just a good thing. So like the myth hadn't penetrated them.

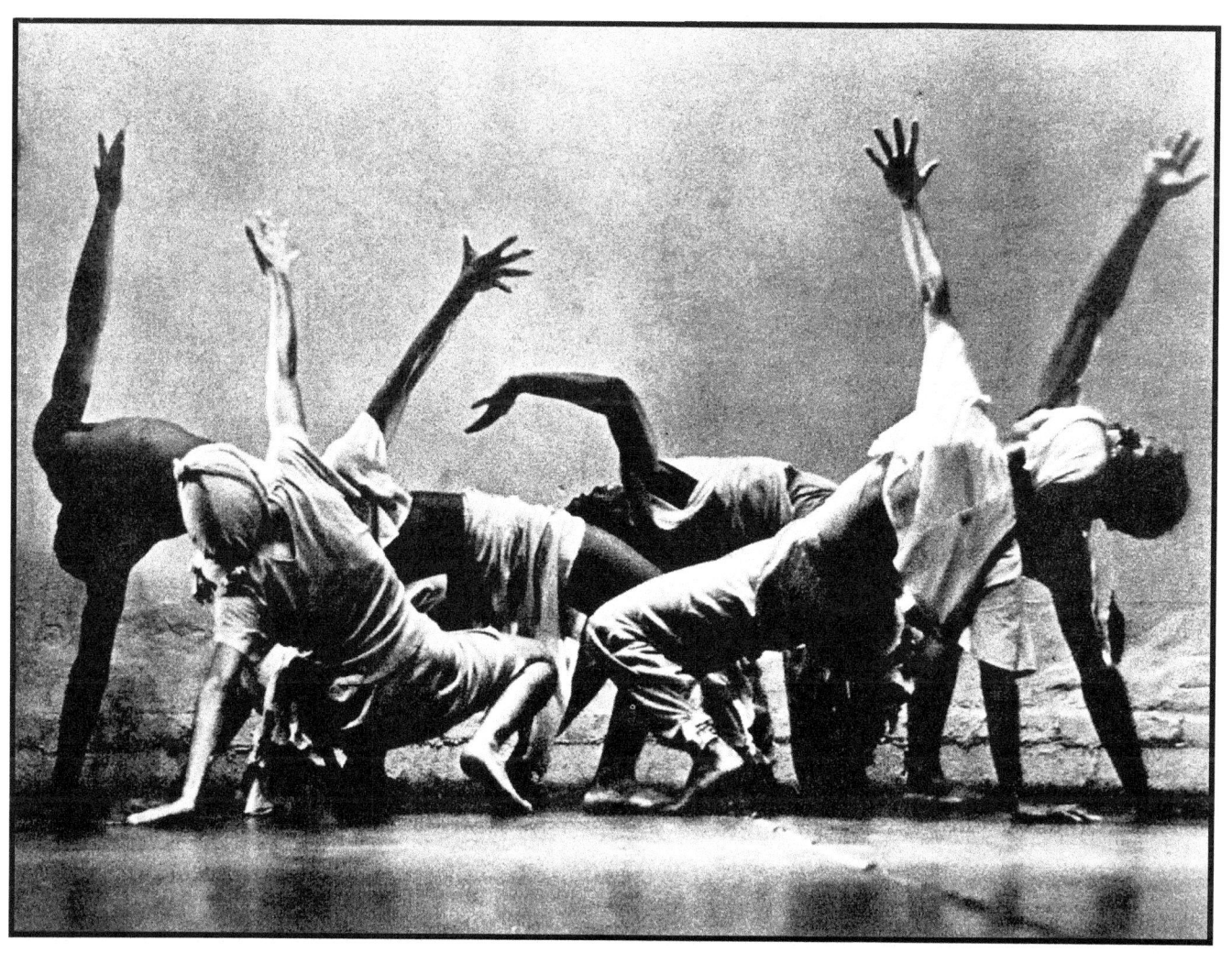

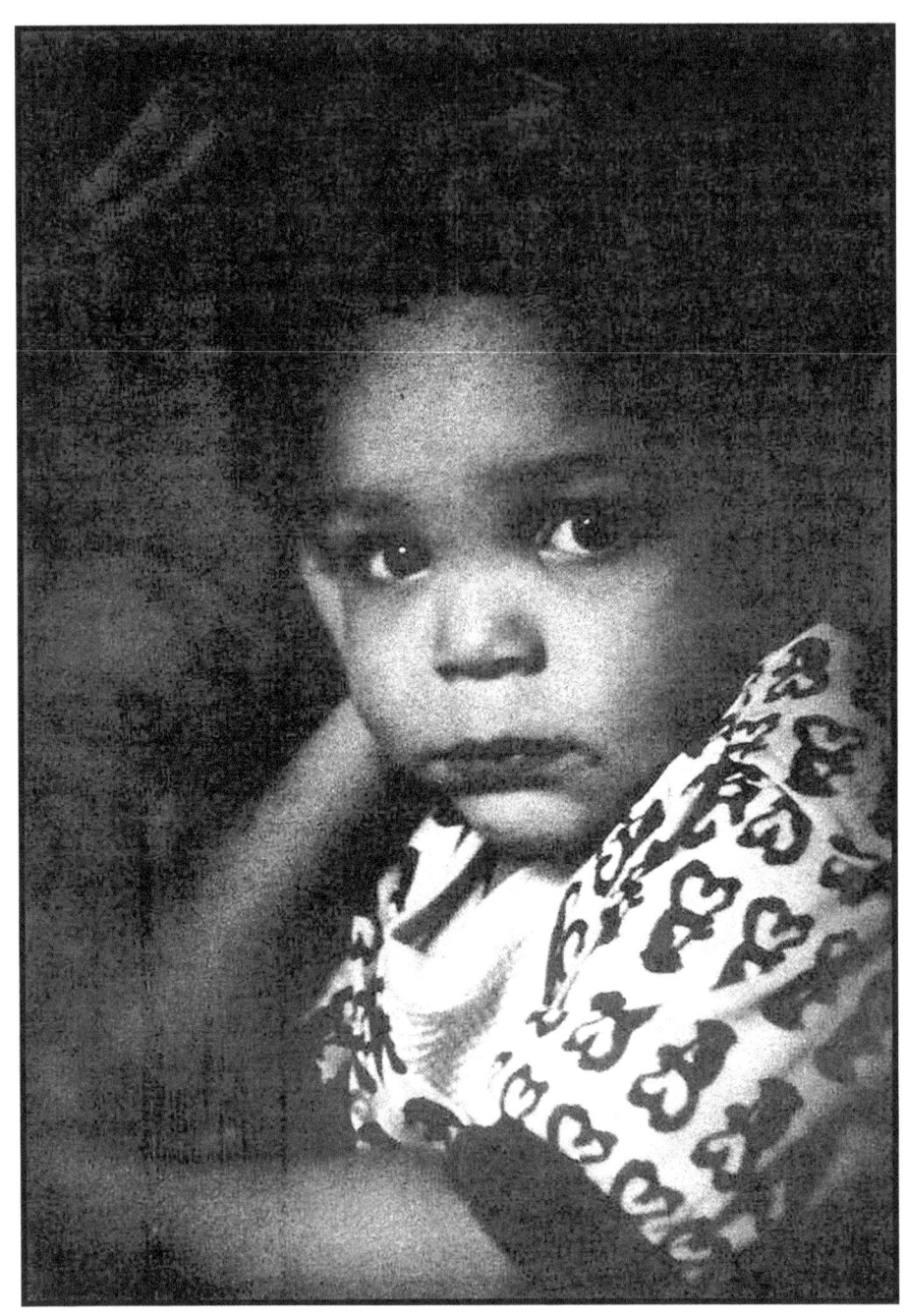

what do you do
when it hurts
real bad?
and there's
no place to go
and no one
to talk to
and you're
unable to
rationalize?
and it hurts
so bad that
your shaking
inside
and your muscles
act crazy
and you can
no longer
deal with people?
when there's beauty
outside
and your heart
is warm
but it won't
stop shaking
and

crying
is not
the black
women's way
of dealing
with her problems?
the children
walk by
and don't even
see them
and you're not
a violent person
the cars go
by
and you wish you
could drive
and there's no
where to run
running would
help
if you could
walk
for miles
and not have
to walk back

and
the man
who hurt you
can't see?

Damany-Kenya Tyson

NUTRITIONAL WELL-BEING

By Brenda Bailey

Many times I walk through the streets of Harlem and feel the misery of ignorance. Ignorance of many things, but mostly ignorance of nutrition and healthy living.

I have rapped to many brothers and sisters about their various diseases and problems only to find that most of these diseases are related to improper nutrition and unhealthy living. We must remember that our external environment is not an optimal one for natural healthy survival. Therefore our internal environment (our bodies) must be. I cannot overemphasize the importance of dealing with nutrition and the science of healthy living to ensure mental, physical and spiritual well-being.

As a minority race we must cope with more tension on a day to day level than any other racial group. A combination of mental well-being and strength is necessary to prevent mental frustration which leads to all types of psychological problems. Proper eating habits combined with good healthy living habits will not only ensure the mind of well-being and strength but will also supply it with positive thought patterns. One cannot expect to have a superior mind when eating inferior foods.

Our physical bodies need an adequate supply of vitamins and minerals to function properly and resist disease. Disease is caused by an accumulation of poisons in the body. If we are to prevent disease, we must learn how to eat and what to eat. Physical energy and extreme tolerance are the results of proper eating habits. Our bodies are temples that must be built and replenished with quality materials.

Spiritual well-being comes from an abundance of mental and physical energy channeled in the proper directions with the proper attitudes. Our spirits cannot be developed when our minds are cluttered with poisons and wastes. Spiritual developement tunes into the forces of nature and beautifies the being.

We must also develop the proper attitude regarding food. Food is a form of nurishment to the body; we must appreciate food for its basic nutritive value. Eating should not be considered a pleasure and consist of poison-ladden foods with little nutritional value. Eating is a functional and basic phase of life, it should be based upon simplicity and quality. Confusion stems from wrong attitudes and misinformation. Eating should have no more emphasis than eliminating; for they are both basic body functions. Meals should be pleasant of course but never as frivolous and complicated as a banquet.

A note about food preparation, food should be prepared in proper utensils and in the manner which will keep the vitamins and minerals in their natural state. The best methods of cooking are baking and steaming (vegetables and fruit) and the best utensils are stainless steel and pyrex. Never use aluminum, for numerous poisons are released into foods when cooking in aluminum pots.

Every family should be into proper nutrition and the science of healthy living to ensure the optimal developement of its members. The science of healthy living is based on the principle of body purification and maintainence through the use of herbs, the natural elements, proper nutrition, exercise, cleanliness, fasts and a positive attitude.

I would like to mention a few places where one can eat and remain in tune with proper nutrition and healthy vibrations. These restaurants are "Health Food" advocates and developed out of a need for clean Healthy eating environments. Some of the finer restaurants include:

Aquarius Health Center
405 West 148th Street
283-8492

The Beautiful Way
149 2nd Avenue
473-9559

Salaam Seven
115 Lenox Avenue
666-1826

Alive Kitchen Restaurant
11West 42nd Street
565-9307

Peace.

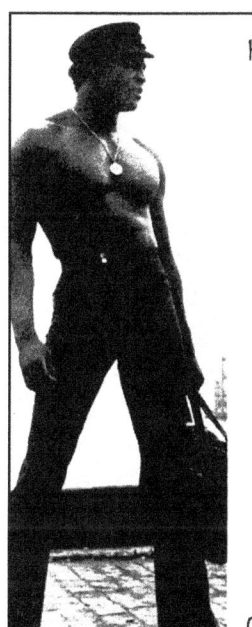
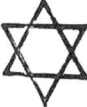
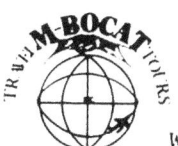
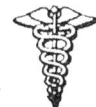
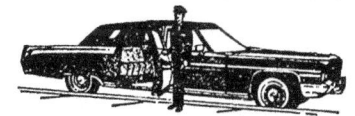

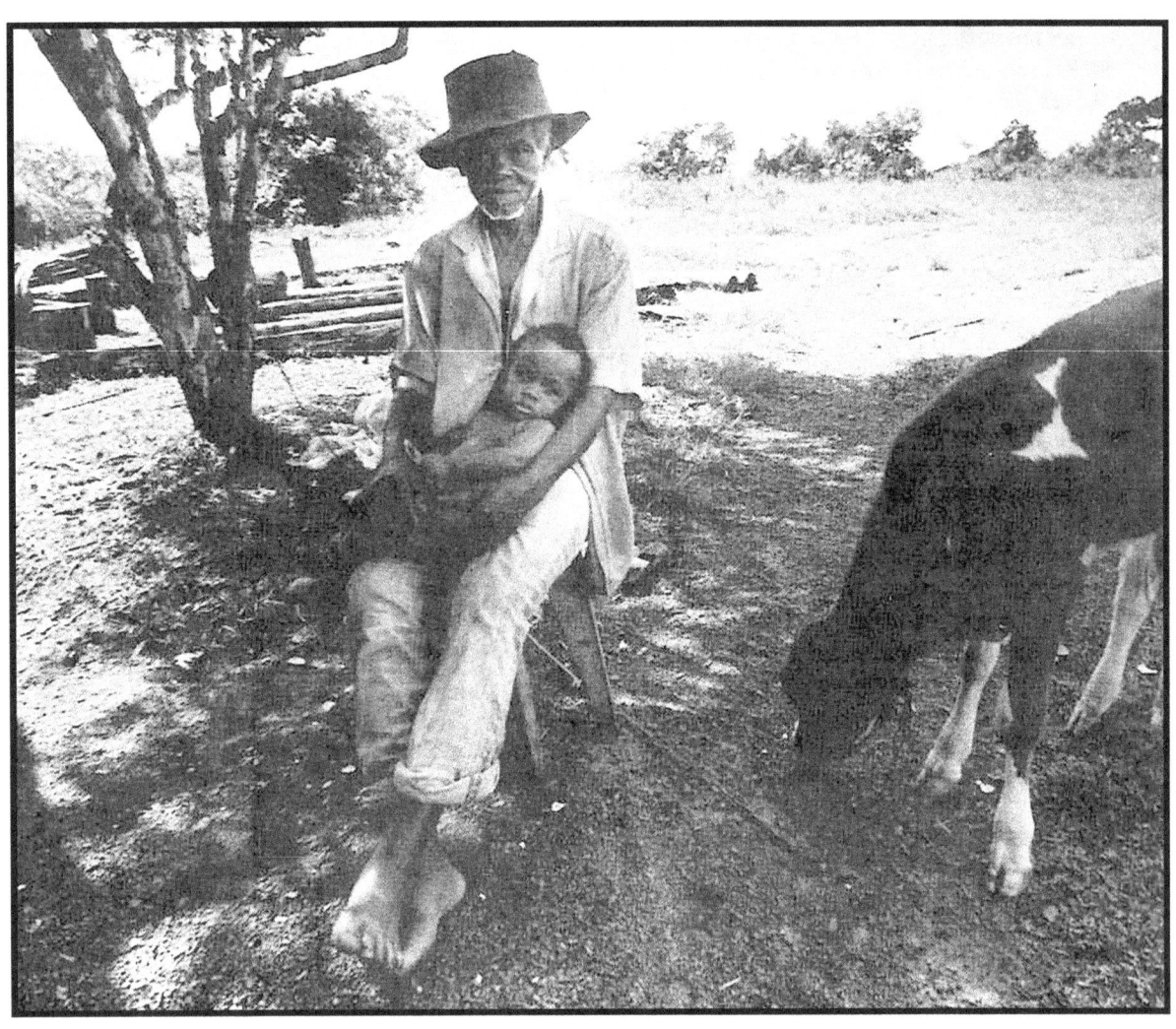

LIFELINES

THEATER REVIEWS

BY CALVIN WILSON

A Hand Is On The Gate

"A HAND IS ON THE GATE," an evening of poetry and music of the Black experience, is an extremely fulfilling theatrical event. Drawing upon the poetry of such great Black writers as COUNTEE CULLEN, LANGSTON HUGHES AND GERALDINE BROOKS, the 127th Street Repertory Ensemble supplements emotionally charged recitations with a background of Black American Music.

Performing in their theatre, (The Afro-American Studio For Acting and Speech), the ensemble maintains a dramatic flow which goes from euphoric choral reading to poignant solo recitations. Sitting in the audience, it becomes impossible not to relate entirely to what's going on up on stage. The set itself is striking in its simplicity and functionality.

"A HAND IS ON THE GATE" gives us a sensitive view of Black History in America: the pain of slavery, the joy of a victory by Jack Johnson, the sweet pleasure of listening to MA RAINEY. The company has managed to avoid the pitfall of poetry becoming boring and preachy when presented dramatically by the use of appropriate music, choreography and by acting out the dynamics of the various poems.

Although the AFRO-AMERICAN STUDIO has been in existence for some time, the repertory company

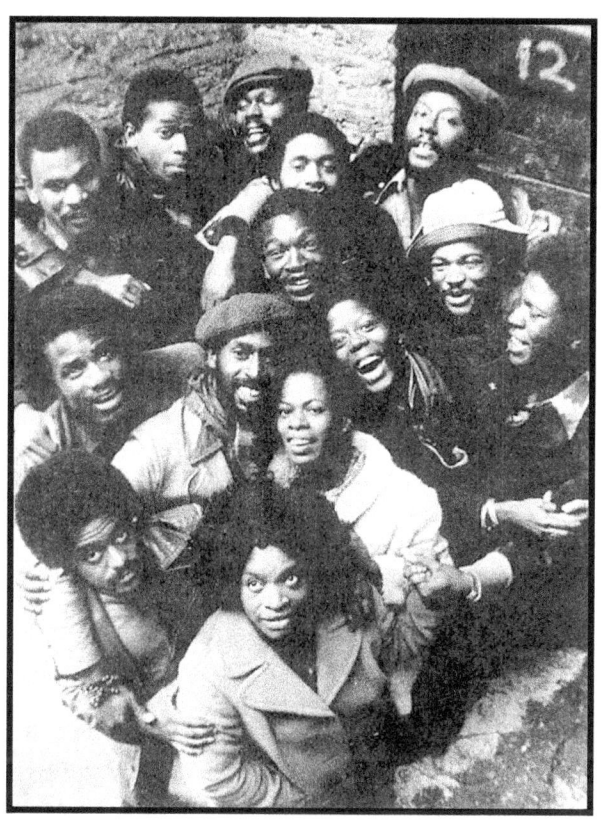

is in its first season. Press agent and actor Lend Wilson attributes the success of the company to two factors: the ability of the members of the company to relate to each other as human beings, which he sees as a product of their constantly working together; and the group's concept of the purpose of Black theater as being to educate Black people to things in our daily lives which we may overlook and in this way help us to grow through learning more about ourselves. The 127th Street Repertory Ensemble has succeeded in its goals, and then some.

The Ups And Downs
Of Theophilus Maitland

Vinnette Carroll and Novella Nelson are two of the most talented people in theatre today. As directors who have also worked as actresses, they both have a total command of theatre both in concept and execution. Part of the reason for this may be found in the use by both directors of the workshop development of a theatrical work.

THE UPS AND DOWNS OF THEOPHILUS MAITLAND, at the Urban Arts Corps Theater, is just such a workshop experience. Although the musical about life in Jamaica is already "finished," director Vinnette Carroll told the audience that she and Micki Grant are still working on it. After this statement was made, the show began. With a book by Carroll and music and lyrics by Grant, THEOPHILUS MAITLAND tells the story of an old man who pursues and eventually weds a young woman, only to find that he's not up to the challenge. All ends happily, however, after many lively dances and songs. A few of the songs are in the reggae style, but most of them could reflect Black Music anywhere. It is, in fact, the universality of the Black experience which comes through most in this play.

Sweet Talk

As much can be said for SWEET TALK, a play by West Indian playwright Michael Abbensetts which was presented in admission-free workshop performances at the Public Theatre. Focusing on the relationship of a Black couple living in a London slum, SWEET TALK deals with their struggle to overcome the tensions brought about by their economic situation. The couple argue and make up, and argue again, secure in the knowledge that they love each other and will stay together. Novella Nelson's direction expressed both the natural humor of daily life and the overall sense of desperation in the environment. The Public Theatre would do well to revive the production at some future date.

Folk shouldn't be put off by the location of the Urban Arts Corps Theatre at 26 West 20th street. THEOPHILUS MAITLAND should definitely be seen, and the subways are still 35¢.

Strivers Row

STRIVERS ROW, a play by Abram Hill, provides us with an interesting and satirical look at the social behavior of middle-class Blacks in the 1940's. In its production at the New Heritage Repertory Theatre, the play achieves a rare and welcome balance between social commentary and high comedy. Moreover, after the struggles of the 1960's, and considering the emerging Black middle class of the 1970's, the play takes on a new relevance.

The play was first produced in the 1940's and is therefore not a nostalgia piece but a record of the time in which it was written. We can see clearly the efforts of a select group of Blacks to affect the materialistic trappings of the white middle class. Still, as the play illustrates, even those who are striving the hardest to get away from their lower-income backgrounds never completely forget where they've come from. The play exposes the differences between success and assimilation and articulates clearly the case for Black awareness of the inequities of the class system.

The tone of the play is immediately set, when we are introduced to Dolly Van Strivens (Zaida Coles) and her maid, Sophie (Claudia Smith). While Dolly tries hard to imitate the traditional role of the "Lady of the Manor," she can never allow herself to treat her maid in the traditional manner. This is made evident when Sophie, noticing that Dolly has removed the "for rent" sign from the front window, puts the sign back in place. Sophie is well aware that the Van Strivens cannot afford the 14 room home they occupy but is also aware of Dolly's need to pretend that the family is better off than it really is.

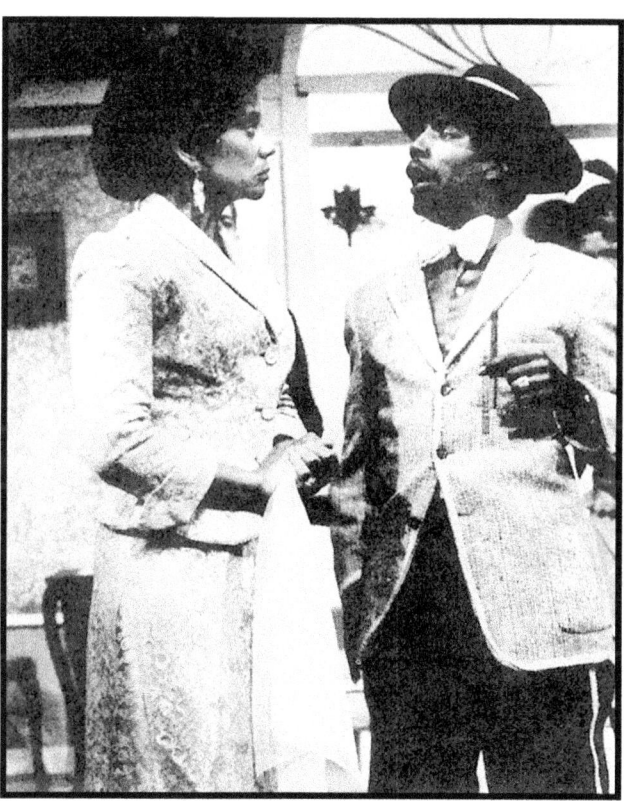

Photo by Gilbert Johnson

The plot, revolving around a coming-out party for Dolly's daughter, is reminiscent of the drawing-room comedy. All of the action takes place in the living room, where several characters at a time wrestle with each other's motivations. Hill's genius is that he has taken this and made it totally workable from a Black perspect-

ive. The drawing-room jokes are there, but they're funky and full of life and have lost none of their punch over 30 years. The characters are fully realized, even though in outline they're only sterotypes. The maid is here, but she's a maid with soul; the middle-class negro playboy is here, but he's a playboy with hang-ups that give him a greater sense of humanity and make us really care what he does and how he feels.

Director Roger Furman deserves praise both for reviving this venerable Black play and for providing it with such a splendid production. The set seems to sit in a limbo between realism and caricature which fits it perfectly. The performances provide an excellent example of ensemble playing. Everyone seems to be pushing personal attention aside in favor of the common cause of entertaining the audience. The entire production moves so well that neither the two intermissions nor the length of the play (two and a half hours, not counting intermissions) is in the least bit annoying. STRIVERS ROW is rich in its understanding of the Black stuggle for economic power and funny in the process.

BUT IT COMES OUT MAD

Sometimes
I just sit down
and
try
to think
of
what it is
I
want to say
to
my man

Don't
want to worry him
about all the troubles
I got
on
my job
because
he ain't workin'

Don't
want to worry him
about
the kids misbehavin'
and
I can't
put no more pressure on that man
about
the bills
we
got to pay

Sometimes
I just
look at my man
'cause I think he's so fine
and I open my mouth to say it
but
it comes out mad

Sometimes
I just take his hand
and
go for a walk
thinkin'
maybe
we can talk
away from everything
but
it
comes
out
mad

When he loves me
I
cry
'cause I really like him
but
I can't tell him so
when he leaves me
I want to
let him know
how much
I
love him
but
I
just let him go
'cause
I know
it
comes out mad

Sometimes
it seems to me
I done already figured out
what it is
I
want to say
to my man

Maybe
tomorrow
I'll figure out

Why
we got to fuss an' fight on Monday
Why
we got to not speak on Tuesday
Why
we got to cut up clothes on Wednesday
Why
we got to throw hot water on Thursday
Why   Why   Why
we got to go-up-side-the-head on Friday

Why   Why
we got to kick ass on Saturday
an'
what's left over
what's left over
How
we got the nerve
to
carry it to Jesus to save
on
Sunday
mornin'

I say
Why
Why
Why
must it always
come
out
mad

Camille Yarbrough

Children Of Mombosa (Kenya)

Photographs by Lloyd DeSuze
and Stan Britt

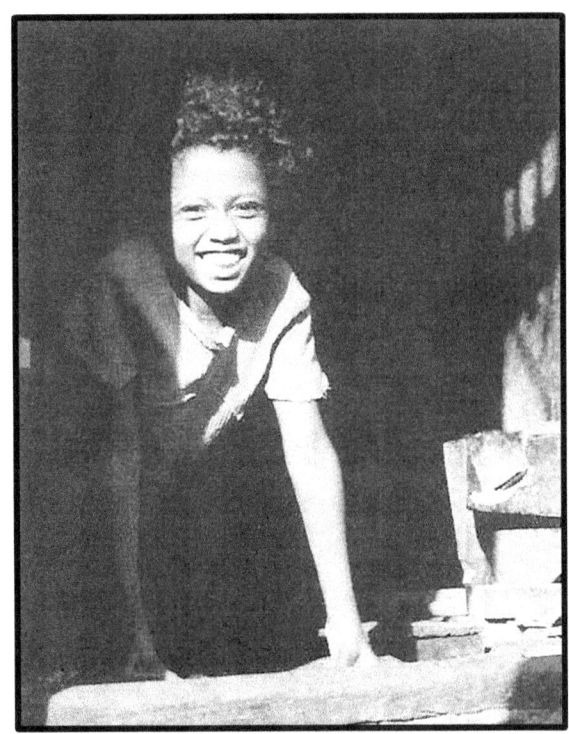

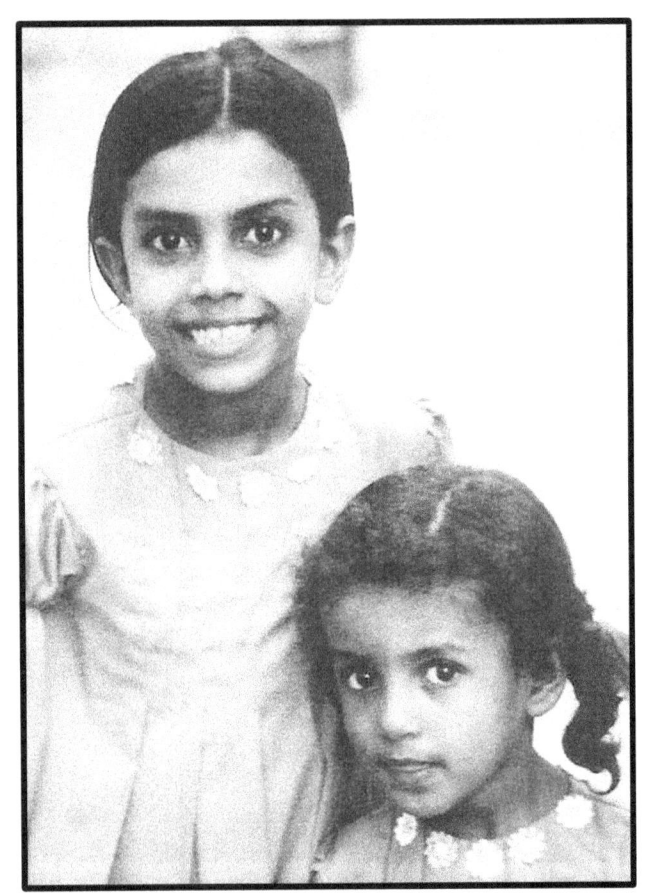

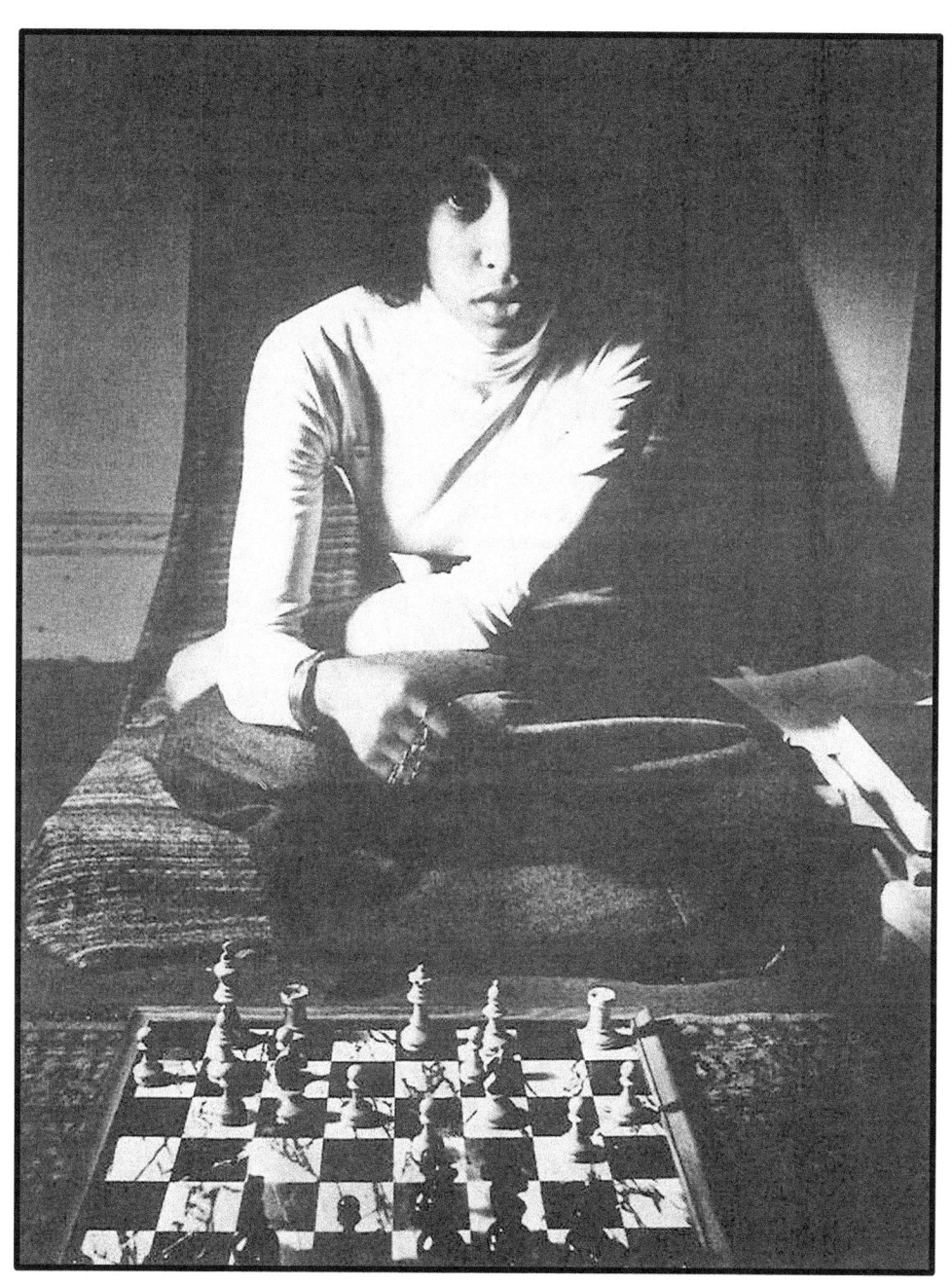

CITY OF CAPITAL

A Temerity that walks
                w
                i
                t
                h populated hatreds

      pur
      suing
appointed legacies-   river of flesh
                      alluvial flower
                      a
                      dull sweat running
                      across the sun
                      maze of water wind
meshing a great distillery
                      of human labor;
city of time courting a patchwork sky,
an azure quilt for the people' sleep
                      sleep of caution
                      created daily
                      the guilt or innocence
                of which languishes in a
                murmur of inertia dredging silence
                      on the
                horizons of downcast eyes
                      traveling
                subway tunnels like sediment in a 9 to 5 dirge
bodies packed
like a grave
            for the masses

cannon of profit
erosion of dawn
a
downtown country that stalks sunlight
like a city discovered with red dust
                      the
                color of war calling
                      out
                the primal thrust to
                heart and a science
that turns plasma to pain
the shape of sky-scrapers and dead men/

                      Baron James Ashanti
                            Harlem
                  October 18, 1974

You asking me 'bout my childhood,
You know how people talk about them was the good ole days,
Well, them was the good ole days,
When life was young, I was young and even Aunt Gin was young back then.
Why every day should have been a warm spring Sunday,
"Cause pure joy was 4th Sunday morning.

Fourth Sunday morning, with Mamma cooking rice and gravy,
Frying pork chops or chicken, hot biscuits dripping with butter,
And Mama's own homemade peach preserves.

Fourth Sunday morning, with Daddy thanking the Lord,
And Mama telling us to hurry,
And Daddy warning us not to be late for church this 4th Sunday morning.
Black patent leather shoes,
Knots being pulled from my hair,
Pretty ribbons tied on my plaits to match my pretty dress,
And vaseline to cover the ash on my legs.
And Dot, Linda, and Daisy dressed all in white,
And me, and Jo, David, and Pat laughing all the way cross town to church,
'Bout everything from our last whipping to Sister Olivia's arm throwing,
Spasmatic shouting.
And Isabella, Sally and Joie walking slowly behind hoping for some
Miracle so that they wouldn't have to go to church this 4th Sunday morning.
And Daddy in place behind the Deacon's row, and Mamma slipping through the church doors,
Just before the choir's processional,
And Roy Jr. sneaking in right after collections, and all us children
Grinning from ear to ear 'cause we knew that Daddy was gonna put one whipping
on his behind.

Fourth Sunday morning, when Rev. Boston stood at the pulpit,
And Deacon Cooper got down on his knees and prayed and prayed and prayed,
'Til it seem like the Lord Himself 'ave to come down and say,
'Son, you don prayed enough.'
Sister Duggins would get up and sing her solo in that high pitched voice,
Jerusalum, Jerusalum, can you imagine listening to that,
With your Mamma and your Daddy staring you dead in the eye,
And daring you to even think a smile,
And it was all I could do to keep from laughing,
But laugh I didn't, 'cause Daddy didn't 'low us to cut up in church.

Fourth Sunday morning,
With Mr. Joe getting up to announce that we would be going to Seaview Beach
On the Sunday school picnic, and
Me wanting to get up and shout,
'Cause the Sunday school picnic was the social outing of the year.
And of course we were told to visit the sick and shut in,
And I never knew how important that was 'til my Daddy got sick with cancer,
And then I knew, I knew why he spent so many 4th Sunday mornings in church,
He called it serving the Lord.

Fourth Sunday morning, when Rev. Boston would get up and preach,
He'd take his text, he'd chant the psalms of David, he'd talk about
Paul and Silas, I remember Moses going down to Egypt and telling
Pharoh to let his people go, he told us about a virgin giving birth
To the Christ child, he hugged the church with the glory of the holy
Ghost, He raved about a time when every day would be Sunday, and
All the saints would go marching in...
'Til Sister Ada could stand it no longer, 'Yes, Lord,' she'd cry,
And then Sister Brown would get up and shout,
'Til the turbulence of Rev. Boston's sermon had calmed like the waves
After a mighty storm, and then
The choir would rock my soul to happiness singing 'Peace Be Still,'
And that night before I went to bed,
I'd thank the Lord for 4th Sunday morning,
And this night before I go to bed,
I'll thank the Lord for 4th Sunday morning.
God Bless you friends,
God Bless you.

Phillis Lu Simpson

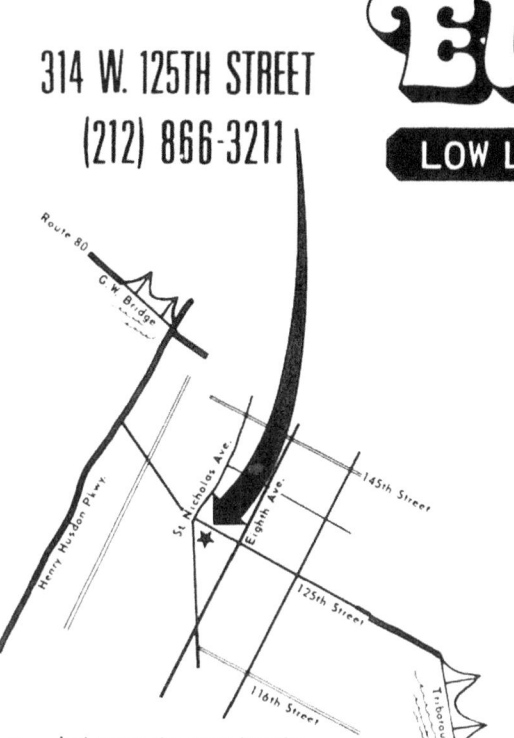

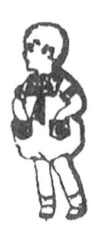

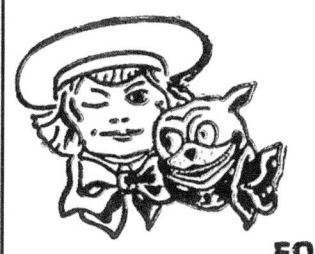
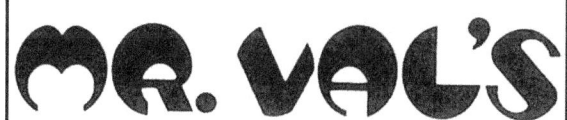
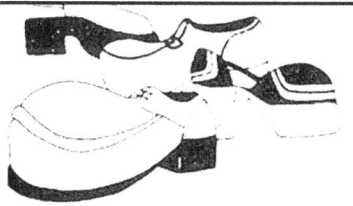

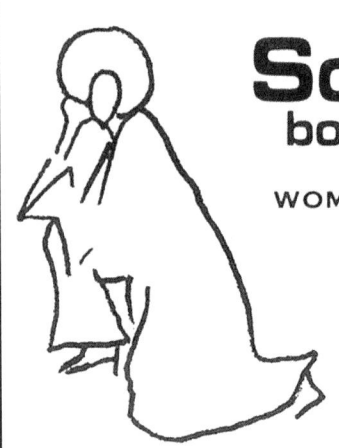
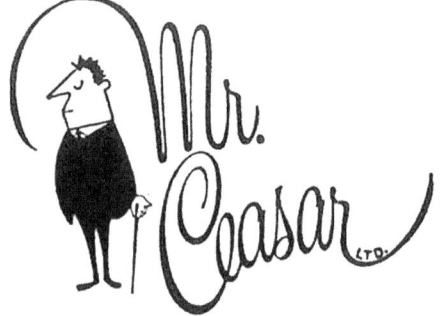
60

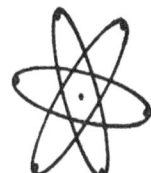

FEDERATION YOUTH PROJECT DIR: GEORGE SAMUELS PRESENTS:

"TELL PHAROAH"   A PLAY BY LOFTON MITCHELL   DIRECTED BY
SAMM WILLIAMS

TOMPKINS PARK PLAYHOUSE
670 LAFAYETTE (BET MARCY & TOMPKINS)   965-6568
DEC. 6   2PM
   7   7:30 PM   ADMISSION FREE
   8   2PM

"THE ISLAND"   WRITTEN BY SOUTH AFRICAN PLAYWRIGHT
ATHOL FUGARD

PRESENTED AT: EDISON THEATER   BOX OFFICE OPENS
240 WEST 47th ST. (bet. B'WAY & 8th)   WEEKDAYS AT 10:00AM
757-7164   SUNDAYS AT 12:00 NOON

SHOWS: WED&SAT 8PM

"SIZWE BENZI IS DEAD"
WRITTEN BY SOUTH AFRICAN PLAYWRIGHT
ATHOL FUGARD

PRESENTED AT: EDISON THEATER
(ABOVE ADDRESS)   SHOWS: TUES,THURS,FRI. 8PM
                                    MAT. WED-2PM
                                    SAT-2PM
                                    SUN-3PM

NEW COMMERCIAL GALLERY OPENING   J.A.M. (JUST ABOVE MID-TOWN GALLERY)
50 WEST 57th STREET
757-3442
COMMERCIAL GALLERY HANDLING BLACK ARTISTS
MONDAY THRU SATURDAY 11AM TO 6PM   CLOSED SUNDAYS

REGGAE CONCERT

DEC. 13 & 14   FRI. 8:00PM   PRICE: $6.00 IN ADVANCE
                SAT. 7:00PM & 11:00PM $7.00 AT THE DOOR

COLUMBIA UNIVERSITY   PURCHASE TICKETS AT: TICKETRON AND
MCMILLIN THEATRE   CARIBBEAN RECORD SHOPS
116th ST. & B'WAY
                         STARRING:
PROMOTER EARL CHIN   HEPTONES   JOHNNY CLARKE
M.C.'S   ALON ELLIS   K.C. WHITE
KEN WILLIAMS W.L.I.B.   AGUSTUS PABLO WILD BUNCH
JEFF BARNES W.W.R.L.

"PEACHES" a new children's book, written and illustrated by Sister DINGA McCANNON
can now be found at most bookstores. Published by Lothrop Lee & Shepard C., 104
Madison Avenue. Price only $4.50

THE HARNESSED AND HARVESTED HISTORY OF BLACK MUSIC IN MOTION IS.....COSMIC COLORS
A BLACK MUSIC MAGAZINE. AVAILABLE AT BLACK BOOKSTORES. FOR MORE INFO. WRITE:
COSMIC COLORS, 1944 MADISON AVENUE. HARLEM, 10035.

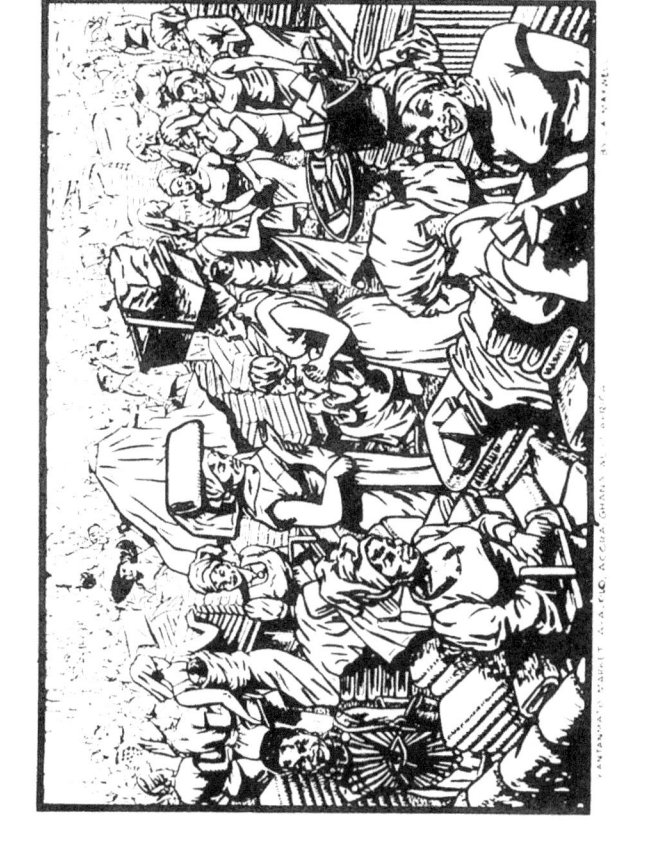
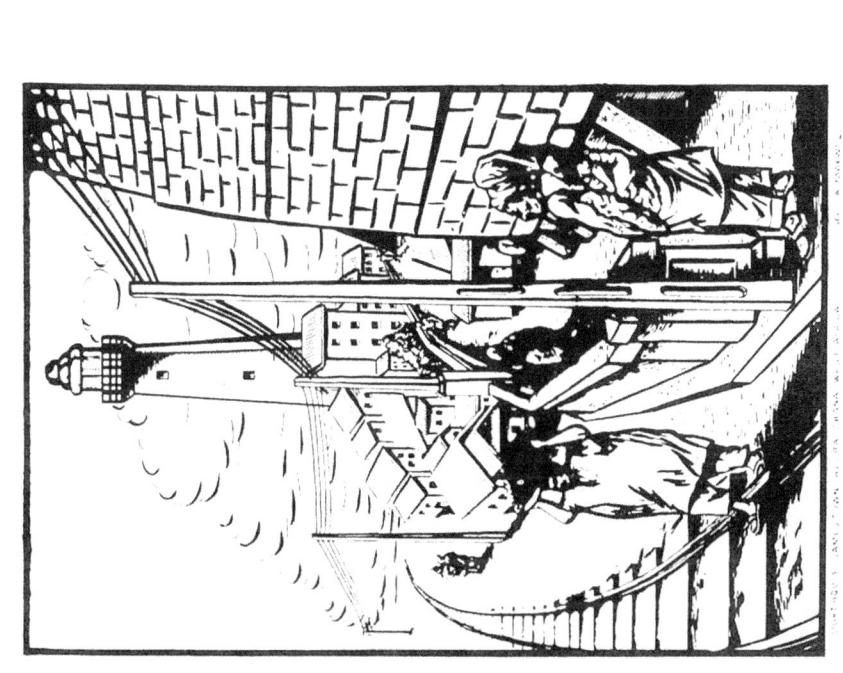

PUBLISHER ACKNOWLEDGEMENTS

The rebirth of the Special 1974 Commemorative Reissue of IMPRESSIONS Magazine of the Arts is a special labor of Love for us. 1974 witnessed an explosion of powerful & creative expressions in: Theater Arts, Poetry, Art, Music, Photography, Literature, Dance / Choreography, Theater Review, Film, Critique, Nutritional Advice & Fashion.

As the independent Publisher of IMPRESSIONS MAGAZINE OF THE ARTS I am very proud to be able to again re-introduce to this new generation, the power and fertile imagination of these generous and talented contributing artists and creators, who worked so hard to honestly represent themselves and their people during this tumultuous, passionate and exciting period.
IMPRESSIONS MAGAZINE is truly a historical and educational snapshot of the times.

LeROY CLARKE
BARON JAMES ASHANTI
ARTHUR FLOWERS
HARRY BELAFONTE
RUFUS BARKLEY
DAVID JACKSON
CALVIN WILSON
ROBERT BOB BRYAN
PAT GLENN
BRENDA BAILEY
MERVYN TAYLOR
DAMANY-KENYA TYSON
CAMILLE YARBROUGH
PHILLIS LU SIMPSON
HERB HENRY
NANCY MILDREN
DESMOND SMITH
TAJ MAHAL
DIANE McINTYRE
MEL WRIGHT
LLOYD DESUZE

GV SERIES IMPRESSIONS Magazine of the Arts Publications

GV16 **IMPRESSIONS Magazine of the Arts (December 1974)** -Reissue Date 09/2012
GV17 **IMPRESSIONS Magazine of the Arts (Spring 1975)** - Reissue Date 10/2012
GV18 **IMPRESSIONS Magazine of the Arts (October 1975)** - Reissue Date 11/2012
GV19 **IMPRESSIONS Magazine of the Arts (June 1976)** - Reissue Date 12/2012

With much love & respect, I sincerely thank you from the top of my heart.

Robert Bob Bryan, Founder / Publisher
Loida Bryan, Co-Executive Producer
website: http://www.graffitiverite.com
e-mail: bryworld@aol.com

.